D0386011

PRESENTED TO:

_____

FROM:

_____

DATE:

_____

Published by Bethany House Publishers
11400 Hampshire Avenue South
Bloomington, Minnesota 55438

Bethany House Publishers is a division of
Baker Publishing Group, Grand Rapids, Michigan

Printed in the United States of America

ISBN-13: 978-0-7642-0287-2
ISBN-10: 0-7642-0287-1

†HE
PRAYER
of
SOLOMON

ENDURING WISDOM FROM
THE WORLD'S WISEST MAN

BETHANYHOUSE
MINNEAPOLIS, MINNESOTA

Solomon's Prayer

At Gibeon the Lord appeared to Solomon in a dream by night, and God said, Ask what I shall give you. And Solomon said, You have shown great and steadfast love to your servant David my father, because he walked before you in faithfulness, in righteousness, and in uprightness of heart toward you. And you have kept for him this great and steadfast love and have given him a son to sit on his throne this day. And now, O Lord my God, you have made your servant king in place of David my father, although I am but a little child. I do not know how to go out or come in. And your servant is in the midst of your people whom you have chosen, a great people, too many to be numbered or counted for multitude. Give your servant therefore an understanding mind to govern your people, that I may discern between good and evil, for who is able to govern this your great people? It pleased the Lord that Solomon had asked this. And God said to him, Because you have asked this, and have not asked for yourself long life or riches or the life of your enemies, but have asked for yourself understanding to discern what is right, behold, I now do according to your word. Behold, I give you a wise and discerning mind, so that none like you has been before you and none like you shall arise after you. I give you also what you have not asked, both riches and honor, so that no other king shall compare with you, all your days. And if you will walk in my ways, keeping my statutes and my commandments, as your father David walked, then I will lengthen your days. 1 KINGS 3:5-14 ESV

Contents

Introduction

Solomon was the wisest man in the world of his time. Many believe that, aside from Jesus, he was the wisest man in the world ever. Since he is known for his remarkable wisdom, the questions beg to be asked: Where did all this great wisdom come from, and how did he receive it?

In 2 Chronicles 1 we are told the reason he received this great wisdom from God was to help him accomplish his purpose and calling to be the king of Israel. In the midst of this wonderful story is a rather obscure prayer that changed Solomon's life. And it has remarkable relevance for us today. It is full of life-changing principles that can help us to live the kind of life we've always wanted—a life that will honor God, influence people for good, and be a difference-maker in this world we live in.

To that end, we offer these insights about one of the greatest prayers in the Bible...the prayer of Solomon. May God reveal His powerful truths to you as you read this book and help you become the person He longs for you to be.

When David's time to die drew near, he commanded
Solomon his son, saying,
"I am about to go the way of all the earth.
Be strong, and show yourself a man,
and keep the charge of the LORD your God,
walking in his ways and keeping his statutes,
his commandments, his rules, and his testimonies,
as it is written in the Law of Moses,
that you may prosper in all that you do and wherever you turn,
that the Lord may establish his word that he spoke concerning me,
saying, 'If your sons pay close attention to their way,
to walk before me in faithfulness with all their heart and with all their
soul, you shall not lack a man on the throne of Israel.'"

1 KINGS 2:1-4

Prologue: The God Who Asks to Be Asked

Then [David] died at a good age, full of days, riches,
and honor. And Solomon his son reigned in his place.

1 Chronicles 29:28

David—Israel's favored king—was dead, and his son Solomon was ruling in his place.

He stood silently before the tabernacle at the great high place at Gibeon. The priests had finally finished their work, and he had sent them away. For the moment, he was alone and all was peaceful.

A slight wind blew, and Solomon watched as it lifted the smoke from the last of a thousand offerings to the Lord. He had prayed and watched as sacrifice after sacrifice was brought to the altar and presented to the Lord. To make so many offerings at once was an extravagance, but it was called for. Without his father for advice, and unsure of whom among his counselors he could fully trust, he had no one to turn to but God.

Anointed by Zadok the priest, and with his throne established according to David's deathbed counsel, Solomon now stood unopposed as the new king of Israel. All those who had rebelled against his father and shed innocent blood in that cause had been executed or exiled. The robes of state lay heavily on Solomon's shoulders. Unconsciously he tugged at them one more time, trying to get used to their weight and authority.

Soon he would leave Gibeon and resume his rightful place on the throne of David's palace. But before beginning the work of his office, he had drawn aside to offer sacrifices of devotion to the God of his fathers. Certainly with the pressing affairs of state, this was not a convenient thing to do. Many might have thought this time better spent evaluating the strength of his armies against the threats of foreign invasion, strategizing plans to govern his kingdom, or calculating the sum of his treasuries. But he did none of these. Instead, he chose to go to the tabernacle and seek God. He knew his father had somehow captured the heart of God and for that reason he himself was blessed—but Solomon wanted to meet the God of David for himself and learn to follow his own path before the Almighty.

To be honest, he was at least a little afraid. The kingdom his father built now lay upon him to rule, judge, and prosper—and Solomon knew the task was too great to handle alone. To rule wisely and justly, he needed God's counsel above all else, and so he had offered a thousand sacrifices and prayed. This costly act of worship would truly mark his kingship and be the foundation of his reign over Israel. God first, no sacrifice too great in His cause, and nothing more important in his heart.

Solomon's gaze followed the rising smoke of the last offering toward heaven. His thoughts turned to Jerusalem, in the rolling hills to the southeast. His father brought the Ark of the Covenant into the city with singing and dancing, but its home was here in the tabernacle. It wasn't right for the ark and the tabernacle to be in separate places, but Solomon knew that his father had never intended for the ark to return here. Instead, it was up to Solomon to build a permanent dwelling place for the ark on a hilltop in Jerusalem. David had left him the plans for the temple and a vast treasury to finance the project.

Now, however, Solomon could do little but stand and wonder what was ahead. He had made the most generous attempt he knew to receive the counsel of the Lord. Conquest, battle, and blood had marked his father's reign; might his be a reign of wisdom, prosperity, and peace?

That night, the Lord came to Solomon to provide the answer.

WORDS TO LIVE BY

priority
1: the quality or state of being prior, first
2: something given or meriting attention before
   competing alternatives

> *Seek first the kingdom of God and his righteousness, and all
> these things will be added to you.* MATTHEW 6:33

motive
something (as a need or desire) that causes a person to
act

> *The aim of our charge is love that issues from a pure heart
> and a good conscience and a sincere faith.* 1 TIMOTHY 1:5

·I·

Beloved of the Lord

*At Gibeon the Lord appeared to Solomon in a dream by
night, and God said, "Ask what I shall give you."*

1 Kings 3:5

That night, as Solomon slept before returning to
Jerusalem, the Lord came to him in a dream.

"Jedidiah."

In his dream, perhaps Solomon heard God call him by
the name He had given him at birth through Nathan the
prophet, which meant "beloved of the Lord."

"Ask for whatever you want Me to give you," God said.

Scripture doesn't tell us that Solomon even stirred, but
somehow in his dream he prayed:

> *You have shown great and steadfast love to your servant
> David my father, because he walked before you in faithfulness,
> in righteousness, and in uprightness of heart toward you. And*

you have kept for him this great and steadfast love and have given him a son to sit on his throne this day. And now, O LORD my God, you have made your servant king in place of David my father, although I am but a little child. I do not know how to go out or come in. And your servant is in the midst of your people whom you have chosen, a great people, too many to be numbered or counted for multitude. Give your servant therefore an understanding mind to govern your people, that I may discern between good and evil, for who is able to govern this your great people?

1 KINGS 3:6-9

This prayer pleased God, so He answered Solomon:

Because you have asked this, and have not asked for yourself long life or riches or the life of your enemies, but have asked for yourself understanding to discern what is right, behold, I now do according to your word. Behold, I give you a wise and discerning mind, so that none like you has been before you and none like you shall arise after you. I give you also what you have not asked, both riches and honor, so that no other king shall compare with you, all your days. And if you will walk in my ways, keeping my statutes and my commandments, as your father David walked, then I will lengthen your days.

1 KINGS 3:11-14

Then Solomon awoke. How he must have wondered at this dream! When all was packed and ready, he and his entourage returned to Jerusalem, and there Solomon stood before the Ark of the Covenant to praise and worship God again with sacrifices of devotion and thankfulness. Then he commanded a feast for all of his court to celebrate God's promises. Solomon—Jedidiah, beloved of the Lord—was ready to face his duties as king of God's people on the earth.

He was his father's choice to be king, and with the Lord's blessing, despite having older brothers in line for the throne, Solomon had a choice as he was crowned king of Israel: pride or gratitude. His actions suggest that he chose to be grateful.

Pulling apart from the politics and hubbub of the capital city, at Gibeon he made his grand gesture of worship and thanksgiving—one thousand sacrifices to the Lord. One thousand sacrifices? One every twenty minutes, twelve hours a day, seven days a week—this could have taken four full weeks! There was no halfheartedness in Solomon's retreat with God.

At this juncture in his life, Solomon had no room in his

heart for arrogance. There were people counting on him—
God's people—and he knew that one day he would be
accountable to God for the stewardship of his calling. Yet
he had also learned from his father that he was not alone
in his responsibility. The God who had called him to be king
was also the God who was willing to enable him to be
king—all Solomon had to do was seek and then follow God's
leading.

GOD ASKS TO BE ASKED

If there is anything about the hustle and bustle of the
pace of our modern life that truly works to squelch our relationship with God, it is that we have so little time to "be
still, and know" that He is God (see Psalm 46:10). So
many aspects of our lives need to be stilled, need to become
reverent, need to be examined. The commute to work that
was once a horseback ride through the woods is today a high-
speed rush with cell phone on and radio blaring the traf-
fic report. Music, television, movies, and computer games
now fill what used to be the silent spaces in our homes. In
contrast, those on the prairie pushing America's borders west-
ward generally had only a handful of books available, and
one of them was always the Bible—kids' play often included

acting out its stories. Today our kids, wired to the world with iPods and cell phones, career from school to dance to soccer to karate to youth group. Being still is just not natural anymore.

This is not a suggestion that we all become Amish, however. The technologies of modern cultural change allow us to accomplish more in our lifetimes than even Solomon, but should we give technological innovations first place—God's place—as the world so often does? Those who follow God have always been called to make choices that go against the flow of culture. We can't afford to merely follow the crowd; God has instead called us to put Him first in spite of external pressures.

GOD DOES NOT FORCE HIS WAY INTO OUR LIVES; HE IS THE GOD WHO ASKS TO BE ASKED.

So, more than any generation that has inhabited the earth before us, we have to choose to take time to pull aside, honor God, pray, and listen for His answers. We can proactively choose to invest time being still before God as Solomon did at Gibeon. God does not force His way into our lives; He is the God who asks to be asked. We have to make the choice to read His Word regularly instead of the latest bestseller. While Solomon had only the early books of the Bible and his father to teach him the statutes and ways of God, we have the full Bible, written for us by over forty of the greatest men of God who have ever walked the earth. In it we have the narratives, letters, visions, poems, songs, and proverbs God recorded for our instruction and so that we can know Him. Just as food is to our bodies, God's Word is to our souls.

KNOWING GOD TODAY

How would you go about getting to know someone famous? You might begin by reading what had been written about this person and what he had written about himself, and the words he had written would be held in higher regard than what others had written about him. Perhaps you would venture to write a letter or send an e-mail asking for a personal explanation of some of what you had read. You would craft that message carefully to ensure a greater likelihood of receiving a response. Then you might call and talk on the telephone, or try to meet in person. The more time you spent with this person, the more you would get to really know him. Eventually you might find yourself listing him as a friend.

Is getting to know God any different? Can it be enough to go to church once a week, listening to what others say about Him? Would you ever count someone as a friend whom you knew by reputation only? Wouldn't you want to spend time one-on-one, talking or corresponding with him yourself?

Solomon had been told about God all of his life and had learned a great deal. No doubt he read as much about God as he could. Yet when it was time for him to begin to rule God's people, he realized he needed to know God more intimately. So he packed his bags and headed for the heights of Gibeon.

He wasn't disappointed.

A DIFFERENT GLIMPSE OF GOD

God is eternal, all-powerful, and all-knowing, so why did He need to appear to Solomon in a dream to ask him what he wished? Didn't God already know? Hadn't Solomon already made it plain while he was offering his one thousand sacrifices? Couldn't God have answered Solomon's prayer even before He heard it?

Of course. But God wanted to meet with Solomon face-to-face even more than Solomon wanted to meet Him!

This may be quite a different glimpse of the God of the Old Testament than you have seen before. We have a tendency to think of Him only as the God who caused the flood, drowned the Egyptian army in the Red Sea, or dealt out any number of other punishments to those who rejected or defied Him. Yet here God comes gently in the night in response to Solomon's earnest seeking, simply to ask what Solomon desired. God didn't even wake him up.

Solomon had gotten God's attention.

Second Chronicles 16:9 tells us that "the eyes of the LORD move to and fro throughout the earth that He may strongly support those whose heart is completely His" (NASB). Whose heart is completely His—isn't that the clincher? How do we prove to God—or is it that we need to prove to ourselves?—that we are truly sincere in being wholly His?

> GOD WANTED TO MEET WITH SOLOMON FACE-TO-FACE EVEN MORE THAN SOLOMON WANTED TO MEET HIM!

For Solomon, it seems to have been the time he spent seeking God and sacrificing to Him at Gibeon. The book of James tells us, "Draw near to God and He will draw near to you" (James 4:8 NASB). This was exactly the principle Solomon applied when he made his thousand sacrifices at Gibeon.

THE BIBLE'S GREATEST PROMISE

Chances are you picked up this book because, like Solomon, you recognize your need for God and you want to draw closer to Him. You want to realize the Bible's greatest promise—that we can know God personally and be His friends—walking with Him like Adam and Eve did in the Garden of Eden, receiving His counsel in our life's calling like Paul, knowing His love and comfort in hardship like David, and knowing His power like Peter and John.

> GOD MAY NEVER APPEAR TO US IN A DREAM, BUT THE BIBLE PROMISES AGAIN AND AGAIN THAT WE CAN KNOW HIM PERSONALLY AND INTIMATELY FOR OURSELVES.

God may never appear to us in a dream, but the Bible promises again and again that we can know Him personally and intimately for ourselves. We can know God's presence in our own lives in the same way we experience relationship with our closest friends, knowing Him even more deeply than did Abraham, Moses, or Solomon!

> "I know the plans that I have for you," declares the LORD, "plans for welfare and not for calamity to give you a future and a hope. Then you will call upon Me and come and pray to Me, and I will listen to you. You will seek Me and find Me when you search for Me with all your heart."
> JEREMIAH 29:11-13 NASB

> Because of Christ and our faith in him, we can now come fearlessly into God's presence, assured of his glad welcome.
> EPHESIANS 3:12 NLT

I love those who love me;
And those who diligently seek me will find me.
PROVERBS 8:17 NASB

This is eternal life, that they know you the only true God,
and Jesus Christ whom you have sent.
JOHN 17:3

The Bible is very clear—as we draw near to God, He will draw near to us.

YOUR OWN THOUSAND SACRIFICES

Seeking God begins by simply calling out to Him to be your Lord and Savior. Because of the death and resurrection of Jesus, no other sacrifices are required. Jesus bridged the gap to God for us, but the Bible says there are offerings you can make to God out of gratitude:

Through him then let us continually offer up a sacrifice of
praise to God, that is, the fruit of lips that acknowledge his
name. Do not neglect to do good and to share what you have,
for such sacrifices are pleasing to God.
HEBREWS 13:15-16

When you speak praises and thanksgivings to God, you offer Him sacrifices.

When you do good to others and share from His bounty in your life to bless others, you offer Him sacrifices.

Obviously, salvation comes by your faith in Jesus as your Lord and Savior, not by your works, but you can present your works to God as love offerings. As William Booth, founder of the Salvation Army, put it, "Faith and works should travel side by side, step answering to step, like the legs of men walking. First faith, and then works; and then faith again, and then works again—until they can scarcely distinguish which is the one and which is the other." Perhaps this is why the Christian way of life is often called the Christian walk.

While there is no magic number as far as offerings are concerned, too often we miss the extravagance that can be shown by simply putting our faith into action. We somehow expect God to reach out to us first so that we can respond; however, He already has—He sent His Son! First John 4:19 says, "We love because He first loved us." Now it is time for us to start relentlessly pursuing God until we see Him sitting on His throne in heaven.

Are you ready to begin that pursuit today? Do you long for God to show up in your life as He did in Solomon's? If so, the best place to begin could be by praying something like this:

A Prayer for Seeking After God

Father,

I want to know you as you promise in your Word. Thank you for sending your Son to save me and your Holy Spirit to guide me in your wisdom. And thank you that you want to know me even more than I want to know you. Thank you for the love you extend to me every day. Father, I want to walk in that love.

I admit that I do not have the wisdom on my own to accomplish all that you have put in my heart to do in this lifetime. I need your guidance to walk every step of every day of my life.

I thank you, too, that you have given me the promises of your Word to accomplish the dreams you have given me, and that I can have confidence that you will do exactly as you have said you will do.

Father, as I read this book and seek you as Solomon did, I ask that you will answer and show up in my life just as you did in his. I also ask that you will show me more clearly your dreams and purposes for my life and that you will give me your wisdom to fulfill all you show me.

I offer my praise and thanksgiving to you and ask these things in Jesus' name.

Amen.

SOLOMON'S LIFE SECRET #1: SEEK GOD

Make pursuing God your priority. Worship Him and ask His direction.

Solomon pulled away from his regular responsibilities to do this. You may not be able to get away right now from the hustle and bustle of your life, but could you forego a favorite TV program to spend time in His Word? Could you take a half-hour walk just to pray and ask for His direction? What else comes to mind that you can do to let God know that you want to make Him your priority and that you long for His guidance in your life?

> *Cry out for insight and understanding. Search for them as you would for lost money or hidden treasure. Then you will understand what it means to fear the LORD, and you will gain knowledge of God.*
> PROVERBS 2:3-5 NLT

Words to Live By

grateful
1a : appreciative of benefits received
 b : expressing gratitude <grateful thanks>

> Let the word of Christ dwell in you richly, teaching and admonishing one another in all wisdom, singing psalms and hymns and spiritual songs, with thankfulness in your hearts to God. COLOSSIANS 3:16

grace
1a : unmerited divine assistance (favor) given man for his regeneration or sanctification
 b : a state of sanctification enjoyed through divine intervention
2: disposition to or an act or instance of kindness, courtesy, or clemency

> If many died through one man's trespass, much more have the grace of God and the free gift by the grace of that one man Jesus Christ abounded for many. ROMANS 5:15

seek
1: to resort to; go to
2: to go in search of; look for

> You who seek God, inquiring for and requiring Him [as your first need], let your hearts revive and live! PSALM 69:32 AMP

· I I ·
BLESSED BECAUSE OF ANOTHER

Solomon said, "You have shown great and steadfast love to your servant David my father."

1 KINGS 3:6

Always dining at King David's table when Solomon was young was a man whose presence there may have been a great curiosity to Solomon. What was this all about? The man was lame—why couldn't he walk? Was he injured in battle trying to protect David? Was that why he now was being shown such honor? Or did David simply feel sorry for him?

Eventually the story would have been told. The man was Mephibosheth, the son of his father's good friend Jonathan. Saul, Jonathan's father—King Saul, the first king of Israel—had tried repeatedly to kill David. When Saul and Jonathan were killed in battle, Mephibosheth was five years old.

David would now be king in Jerusalem, and Saul's servants rushed to escape the city, fearing David would slay them all and Mephibosheth as well. In the chaos of their flight, a nurse dropped Mephibosheth, and both his feet were badly injured.

Some years after David was established as king, he longed to bless someone for the sake of Jonathan, and he learned that Jonathan's son was still alive. David commanded that Mephibosheth be brought to him at once. He restored all the lands of Saul to Mephibosheth and commanded that for the rest of his days, Mephibosheth would be a royal guest at David's table.

Solomon must have wondered at the fact that this man, through no merit of his own, was blessed beyond any warrior who had fought beside David in any battle. Mephibosheth was blessed for the sake of another. It was a principle that would replay itself in Solomon's life as well.

As Solomon grew older, he must also have begun to notice the murmurs that surrounded his mother—the looks, the jeers, the conversations that stopped abruptly as she walked into the room with her son at her side. Eventually, he must have asked his mother about it and been told, when Bathsheba felt he was old enough, the story of how she came to be queen of Israel. Her relationship with David had begun in adultery, and David had ordered her husband killed in battle to cover for her pregnancy. Although she was married to David by the time of the birth, God knew the truth and sent Nathan the priest to confront David about his sin. Despite David's repentance in sackcloth and ashes, the child, Solomon's older brother, died in infancy. The whole affair had ushered a sword of rebellion into David's reign, and two of David's other sons—Amnon and Absalom— also died as a result.

But the story didn't end there. Out of David and Bathsheba's union had also come forgiveness and grace. "You see," Bathsheba might have told Solomon, "our God is not only a God of justice but a God of mercy as well. God deeply loves your father, and your father deeply loves me, despite all the death and trouble that has come of our relationship. Our God is a God of redemption. So it was that when you were born, Nathan the prophet came to us with a word from God. God said that your name would be Jedidiah, 'beloved of the Lord.' You, my son, over all your older brothers, will be the next king of Israel. Where sin once

SOLOMON KNEW HE WAS JUST LIKE MEPHIBOSHETH— BLESSED NOT FOR HIMSELF, BUT BECAUSE OF ANOTHER.

abounded, now there is grace that abounds even more.

"While some people judge your father only by his mistake, God has forgiven him because he has always been a man quick to repent, faithful to God's intentions, and dedicated to God's ways. When God looks at him, He doesn't see sin but a heart hungry to please Him and a man of integrity and honor who will not turn away from God's commandments, no matter the personal price. This is your legacy, and if you embrace it, you will be richly blessed."

When the God and Creator of the universe told Solomon, "Ask what I shall give you," Solomon's first response was to acknowledge his father's faithfulness and integrity that now allowed Solomon this place of favor as king over Israel:

> *You have shown great and steadfast love to your servant*
> *David my father, because he walked before you in faithful-*
> *ness, in righteousness, and in uprightness of heart toward*
> *you. And you have kept for him this great and steadfast love*
> *and have given him a son to sit on his throne this day.*
> 1 Kings 3:6

When God came to Solomon to bless him with what his heart desired, Solomon's first words acknowledged that he knew God's offer was not made because of who he was or anything he had ever done. No, God's offer came because of who Solomon's father was and what David's relationship with God had been. Solomon knew he was just like Mephibosheth—blessed not for himself, but because of another.

A QUESTION OF RELATIONSHIP

In Hebrew, the word for "steadfast love" is *checed*, most often used in the Old Testament to express the active good-will and attitude of mutual blessing that exists between covenant partners. It describes the feeling and obligation of mutual blessing found between a husband and wife, two families joined through marriage, or two profound friends.

Traditional marriage vows are the strongest pledge of union possible between two people. Bride and groom pledge their futures together "for better, for worse; for richer, for poorer; in sickness and in health; to love and to cherish till death do us part, according to God's holy ordinance; and thereto I plight thee my troth." That last phrase means "I pledge to you my most solemn vow and trust you to do so as well." No matter what the future might hold, the bride and groom are melding their destinies for the rest of their lives and promising to do all within their power to protect, provide for, and support one another, no matter the consequences. The marriage covenant is "sealed" with wedding rings—unbroken circles representing the enduring effect of the agreement. "Wherefore they are no more twain, but one flesh. What therefore God hath joined together, let not man put asunder" (Matthew 19:6 KJV).

Early in his friendship with David, Jonathan gave David four symbolic gifts:

> As soon as he had finished speaking to Saul, the soul of Jonathan was knit to the soul of David, and Jonathan loved him as his own soul. . . . Then Jonathan made a covenant with David, because he loved him as his own soul. And Jonathan stripped himself of the robe that was on him and gave it to David, and his armor, and even his sword and his bow and his belt.
>
> 1 SAMUEL 18:1, 3-4

Each gift had a significant meaning. Imagine Jonathan saying, "I give you my coat in pledge that as long as I have a coat to share, you will have one too. I give you my armor in pledge that my protection will be your protection. My sword is yours to attack your enemies. My bow [Jonathan was a skilled bowman] is yours to show that my strengths and skills are yours to meet your needs. My belt is yours to show that I will always uphold you in truth and support you in whatever you do."

It was because of his relationship with Jonathan that David, once he was king, so blessed Mephibosheth when he found him. And Solomon realized that he was being blessed because of David's relationship with God. Whatever Solomon might request, God would give him, for the sake of his father David. Because of David, Solomon could stand before the King of kings and make his petitions known.

WHAT'S IN A NAME?

As Christians we can emulate Solomon's attitude. And we have all the more reason to, because our covenant with God is greater than Solomon's.

The night before He went to the cross, Jesus said:

> No longer do I call you servants, for the servant does not know what his master is doing; but I have called you friends, for all that I have heard from my Father I have made known to you.
> JOHN 15:15

He also said:

> Truly, truly, I say to you, whatever you ask of the Father in my name, he will give it to you. Until now you have asked nothing in my name. Ask, and you will receive, that your joy may be full.
> JOHN 16:23-24

And in John 17:26 Jesus said:

> *I made known to them your name, and I will continue to make it known, that the love with which you have loved me may be in them, and I in them.*

To this point, Jesus' relationship with His disciples was as a master to servants, but now, He told them, things would be different. Like David and Jonathan, Jesus and His followers would be joined in a covenant relationship where each pledged himself to the success of the other. Jesus had a mission, a calling, a purpose for each of them to fulfill, and He was putting all His resources—His wisdom, His foresight, His faith, His power, and His authority—behind them for their success. Now that Jesus was going to the cross to fully open heaven again so that God's kingdom could reign on earth—that His "will be done, on earth as it is in heaven" (Matthew 6:10)—He was looking for friends and partners to actively pursue His goals and dreams while being in constant communication with Him.

PERHAPS WE MAKE A MISTAKE OF ENDING PRAYER "IN JESUS' NAME" INSTEAD OF BEGINNING WITH IT.

Not only are Jesus' followers called into covenant relationship with God but each of us is also given Jesus' name—

His authority—in which to pray. In a sense, Solomon prayed in the name of his father: "Lord, you loved my father David so much, and I know it is why you are here." When we pray in Jesus' name, we are saying something similar: "Lord, we know our prayers have your ear because of who Jesus is and because of His faithfulness, righteousness, and uprightness of heart before you." Perhaps we make a mistake of ending prayer "in Jesus' name" instead of beginning with it. In essence, every time we come to prayer, we should remember:

> Since then we have a great high priest who has passed through the heavens, Jesus, the Son of God, let us hold fast our confession. For we do not have a high priest who is unable to sympathize with our weaknesses, but one who in every respect has been tempted as we are, yet without sin. Let us then with confidence draw near to the throne of grace, that we may receive mercy and find grace to help in time of need.
> HEBREWS 4:14-16

REDEMPTION BEYOND REASON

As news spread that David was on his deathbed, some in David's court prepared to proclaim David's son Adonijah king. But God had different plans.

After David's adultery with Bathsheba and his subsequent murder of her husband, it is amazing to think that not only did God allow David's marriage to Bathsheba to stand but He also allowed one of their sons to become part of the line through which Jesus would be born generations later. There is no greater example in the Bible of the redemptive nature of God's forgiveness than this, other than the transformation of Saul the persecutor into Paul the apostle.

Some scholars have suggested that Solomon's kingship resulted from manipulation by Nathan the prophet and Bathsheba, but there is evidence in Scripture that Solomon was indeed God's choice. Solomon is the only son of David to whom God gave a special name. The Bible portrays Nathan as a man of courageous moral fiber as well as a man who heard clearly from God. God sanctified Solomon's kingship through His appearance to him at Gibeon and offering to grant whatever Solomon requested. And Jesus came through Solomon's lineage.

These four facts taken together indicate that it was Solomon God wanted on David's throne and no other. From David's greatest sin came the first part of the fulfillment of God's greatest promise to him—that he would have an heir on the throne of Israel forever. What must it have been like for Solomon to know that God had made him king of Israel because of His love for David, even though David had other sons more properly in line for the throne? What is it like to receive from God far greater than we can ask or imagine and for no merit of our own?

But of course, if we have been born again, we know the answer to that!

Pray as Children of the King

Realizing all we have received because Jesus is our covenant representative with the Father impacts how we pray. Before Solomon said anything to God about his own desires, Solomon praised God's steadfast love for David that was now blessing him. In the same way, God hears and answers us not because of who we are or what we have done but because of the faithfulness and righteousness of Jesus and what He has done. Our only place for confidence is Christ. When we accept Him as Lord and Savior, the same favor that God has for Jesus falls on us for His sake—and as a result we have access to all of heaven as Jesus' representatives on earth.

> *This is the confidence that we have toward him, that if we ask anything according to his will he hears us. And if we*

> *know that he hears us in whatever we ask, we know that we*
> *have the requests that we have asked of him.*
> 1 JOHN 5:14-15

One often-overlooked aspect of praying "according to his will" is acknowledging what Jesus did to earn us access and the right to come boldly to our Father with our requests. From Solomon we can learn that gratitude and humility are the entry point for all our requests to God, not because we have earned the right to ask, but because Jesus has:

> *Christ Jesus is the one who died—more than that, who was*
> *raised—who is at the right hand of God, who indeed is inter-*
> *ceding for us. Who shall separate us from the love of Christ?*
> ROMANS 8:34-35

To belittle this reward of fellowship with Christ is to despise what Jesus did to win it, just as rejecting the throne of Israel by Solomon would have been to scorn what his father did to establish and solidify it.

Prayer is not about elegant words spoken for all to hear but about God's children earnestly expressing themselves to the Father. Are your prayers filled with gratitude and faith, or are they prayers of last resort? Do you acknowledge only your own needs and desires, or do your prayers also reflect your responsibility and calling to expand the kingdom of God on earth? Do you pray in despair, wondering if God will hear and consider your requests, or do you pray realizing that by the mention of Jesus' name your requests are top priority at the throne of God? Do you pray as a beggar hoping for enough to make it through the day, or do you pray with the grateful attitude of a son or daughter of the King?

REALIZING ALL WE HAVE RECEIVED BECAUSE JESUS IS OUR COVENANT REPRESENTATIVE WITH THE FATHER IMPACTS HOW WE PRAY.

A COVENANT PRAYER

Father,

Thank you for the privilege of being "in Christ" through His sacrifice as my covenant representative to heaven, and that I have the right to pray to you in His name, making my requests known to you that my joy on earth will be full. I realize that I can love you and pray to you because you first loved me and sent Jesus to earth to redeem me. Lord, I am more grateful for this than I can express.

Teach me to pray as I should. Show me from your Word the power of prayer and what it is I should be praying for. Help me understand my calling and the purpose for which you put me on the earth so that I can fulfill your plan for me.

Thank you for your Son and what He did for me so that I can live in your promises and have access to your throne through prayer. May I never forget or take for granted all that this means.

Amen.

SOLOMON'S LIFE SECRET #2:
PRAY CONFIDENTLY

Solomon knew that God's blessing was upon him because of his father David's relationship with God. Because of David, God accepted and blessed Solomon as well.

If you are a Christian, God accepts you and blesses you because of Jesus. God knew you could never be perfect, so Jesus lived the perfect life on your behalf. And you now have access to come before God's throne and make your petitions because the favor God bestowed upon Jesus has been transferred to your account. Obviously, this doesn't give you license to live a sinful life; on the contrary, it should humble you and make you grateful for all He has done.

Are you freely and confidently going to the Father with all your needs, struggles, and decisions?

> *Therefore, brethren, since we have confidence to enter the holy place by the blood of Jesus . . . let us draw near with a sincere heart in full assurance of faith.*
> HEBREWS 10:19, 22 NASB

WORDS TO LIVE BY

covenant

1: a usually formal, solemn, and binding agreement;
compact

2: a relationship of love and loyalty between the Lord
and His chosen people

> *Incline your ear and come to Me.*
>
> *Listen, that you may live;*
>
> *And I will make an everlasting covenant with you*
>
> *According to the faithful mercies shown to David.*
>
> ISAIAH 55:3 NASB

forgive

1a : to give up resentment of or claim to requital for; <for -
give an insult>

 b : to grant relief from payment of; <forgive a debt>

2 : to cease to feel resentment against (an offender);
pardon <forgive one's enemies>

> *For as high as the heavens are above the earth,*
>
> *so great is his steadfast love toward those who fear him;*
>
> *as far as the east is from the west,*
>
> *so far does he remove our transgressions from us.*
>
> PSALM 103:11-12

· III ·

A Man After God's Own Heart

He walked before you in faithfulness, in righteousness,
and in uprightness of heart toward you.

1 Kings 3:6

Imagine how it might have happened . . .

With his mother, Bathsheba, at his side, young Solomon walked apprehensively into the council chambers of the palace. It wasn't often his father had time to see him, but today David had requested a special audience with his son.

David looked haggard and weary from little sleep. His robes were still torn at the neck and his cheeks wet with tears. Absalom's rebellion had put the kingdom into turmoil, but now David and those who remained of his family had returned to Jerusalem and reclaimed the palace. It was not, however, a joyous occasion because Absalom, David's son and one of Solomon's older brothers, was dead.

Despite his grief, David smiled when he turned and saw Solomon. "My son," he said, taking the young man into his arms.

David gave Solomon the chair where he himself often sat to ponder the counsel of his advisors. The gesture made no small impression on Solomon. Then David paced before him and began to speak. It was as if, in one session together, David longed to put into Solomon's heart all that he had failed to teach Absalom, not because he feared another rebellious son but because he longed for Solomon to live fully and one day take his throne.

Solomon leaned forward, his eyes fixed on his father. He would remember all his father had to tell him, and someday he would write it down: "Hear, O sons, a father's instruction, and be attentive, that you may gain insight, for I give you good precepts; do not forsake my teaching.... 'Let your heart hold fast my words; keep my commandments, and live'" (Proverbs 4:1-2, 4).

Likely there were other days like that one as well—days when the teaching of his father burned into Solomon's heart to become the foundation for Solomon's reign and all his writings. But nothing would surpass this first teaching, drawn from the example of David's own life of integrity.

Passion for God

The Bible presents few characters in as much detail as it does David. Scripture clearly presents David as a human being comprised of both frailties and strengths. It is as if God went to extra lengths to show us through David's story what we could be in spite of our own shortcomings.

What was it about David that so captured God's heart?

He was at the same time a warrior, a musician, a poet, an adulterer. He ruled by the sword. At times he let his own authority go to his head. He seems a poor father, whose children openly rebelled against him. Hardly commendable, godly traits! Yet there was something about David that God treasured and that Solomon took to heart.

If we were to choose one word to express who David was, it would probably be passion. He lived a life of passion after God; he fought with passion against God's enemies; he wrote passionate psalms of praise, worship, and repentance.

He failed because of his passion for another man's wife, but his redemption came because of the passion of his repentance before God when he was confronted with his sins. David also carried an incredible passion for building God a permanent dwelling place among His people in Jerusalem, and he stored up incredible resources toward a temple he knew would not be built during his lifetime. And when his son Absalom was killed in the midst of attempting to take the throne from his father, David carried great passion for his son, mourning that it was he, and not David himself, who had to die. (See 2 Samuel 18:33.)

Besides David's passion for God, Solomon identified three other characteristics of David's life that mattered to God: faithfulness, righteousness, and an upright heart. For Solomon, these three traits were the reason God showed such great and steadfast love to his father.

Unwavering Faith

Picture David as a youth, before he was anointed to be king by the prophet Samuel. He's a boy with a harp, singing to the Lord as his sheep graze alongside a gurgling stream. See David the psalmist, spending hours with God in worship and prayer and writing songs about his experiences. Watch him dance for joy without his kingly robes before the Ark of the Covenant as it is brought into Jerusalem. David the God chaser.

After he was anointed king and while King Saul was still alive, however, David was not without enemies. Read Psalm 23 and imagine David hiding in a cave with his men posted at the entrance, watching for the army that was searching to destroy him.

> *The LORD is my shepherd; I shall not want.*
> *He makes me lie down in green pastures.*
> *He leads me beside still waters.*
> *He restores my soul.*
> *He leads me in paths of righteousness for his name's sake.*
>
> *Even though I walk through the valley of the shadow of death, I will fear no evil,*
> *for you are with me; your rod and your staff,*
> *they comfort me.*
>
> *You prepare a table before me*
> *in the presence of my enemies;*
> *you anoint my head with oil; my cup overflows.*
> *Surely goodness and mercy shall follow me*
> *all the days of my life,*
> *and I shall dwell in the house of the LORD forever.*
> PSALM 23

David was confident of the Lord's promises. He experienced God's presence and strength when he fought the lion and the bear threatening his sheep and when he killed the giant Goliath. He knew he could rely on God, and for this reason he never lost faith in Him, even when his circumstances looked their worst.

David's heart cry was always for more of God.

Despite his own frailties or life's letdowns, David didn't waver in his relationship with the Lord. In the quiet meadow, he prayed and praised; in the desert cave, he prayed and praised; in the palace, he prayed and praised; on the run from a rebellion led by his own son, he prayed and praised; and when he sinned, he repented, prayed, and praised.

> DAVID'S HEART CRY WAS ALWAYS FOR MORE OF GOD.

David's faithfulness was marked by passion never to be without God in any decision or circumstance of life. It is not hard, then, to see why goodness and mercy followed him all the days of his life.

LETTING GOD BE GOD

Because David knew he could rely on God and on God's promises, he refused to take his cause into his own hands. In 1 Samuel 24, we are told how Saul heard of David's location and pursued him with three thousand handpicked soldiers. Along the way, Saul took time out to relieve himself in a cave, not knowing that David and his men were actually hiding from him in the depths of that same cave.

BECAUSE DAVID KNEW HE COULD RELY ON GOD AND ON GOD'S PROMISES, HE REFUSED TO TAKE HIS CAUSE INTO HIS OWN HANDS.

Surely, said David's men, here was a God-given opportunity—Saul was defenseless, with his guards outside the cave. All David needed to do was sneak up and quietly dispose of the man who had sworn repeatedly that he would not rest until David was dead.

David did cut off a corner of Saul's robe, which he used later as proof that he had been there and could have killed Saul easily but refused to do so. Guilt overtook David even at so harmless an act, however. He told his men:

> The LORD forbid that I should do this thing to my lord, the LORD'S anointed, to put out my hand against him, seeing he is the LORD'S anointed.
> 1 SAMUEL 24:6

Nor would David allow any man who served in his army to harm Saul.

Had he been willing to kill Saul there in the cave, David could have taken the throne of Israel, which he knew was rightly his. But he refused to force his way by his own strength into what God had promised. He knew that if he did, he would be on his own and would fail as king, just as Saul failed when he chose to act according to his own counsel rather than follow God's clear instructions. Saul had looked to men to establish his throne; David would look to no one but God.

Even when his son Absalom rebelled against him, David refused to act in his own defense but fled Jerusalem before Absalom captured the city. If God wanted David to remain king over His people, then God was big enough to take care of it. If He did not, then David would live as an exile as he had in the days of Saul—David had done it before; he could do it again. But whatever he did, he would not violate his conscience in such matters.

David consistently chose to do what was right in spite of how he might suffer. How this kind of faith must have touched the heart of God!

STAYING RIGHT WITH GOD

When the Ark of the Covenant came into Jerusalem, David danced like a fool before it, celebrating what God had done for Israel like any other common citizen. His wife

Michal rebuked him for not acting properly as a king, for he was "uncovered" in her sight (see 2 Samuel 6:20) without his kingly robes. But David cared more about what God thought than what Michal thought. His focus was on pleasing and celebrating God, not anyone else.

When the prophet Nathan went to David and confronted him about his sin with Bathsheba and his subsequent murder of her husband, Uriah, to cover up his adultery, David was deeply convicted. He didn't make excuses to avoid his guilt or cry for Nathan to forgive him; instead he repented before God. He then fasted and prayed for seven days in the hope that God might save the life of his illegitimate child.

Earlier, when the prophet Samuel had confronted Saul in a similar way about his disobedience, Saul made excuses and then asked Samuel to forgive him. The conviction of Saul's heart was to please only himself or others, not God, and for this God removed him as king. David, however, remained king until his death, and God was true to his promise that if David's sons followed his example there would be an heir of David on the throne of Israel forever. Ultimately Jesus, the King of kings who will reign over God's people forever, was born from the lineage of David.

David let his stories be truthfully told; his prayer of

repentance is found in Psalm 51. He knew that our sin is not an insurmountable problem for God but refusing to fellowship with Him is. As it is often said, "It is all about who you know." When you decide that nothing will keep you from knowing God with all your heart, nothing can stand between you and where God wants you to be.

> HE KNEW THAT OUR SIN IS NOT AN INSURMOUNTABLE PROBLEM FOR GOD BUT REFUSING TO FELLOWSHIP WITH HIM IS.

THE NECESSITY OF INTEGRITY

When a builder plans to construct a skyscraper, one of his concerns is the structural integrity of the steel that will be used, as well as the structural integrity of the building's design and frame. Structural integrity is determined by the purity of elements going into the steel, the quality of the manufacturing process for that steel, and the ability of the structure to bear the load required.

In a structure with low integrity, it is quite possible for the problem to go unnoticed for years until some unusual pressure or load is applied—then the faulty construction tumbles to the ground. But the greater the integrity, the more weight and "responsibility" the steel can handle. In a similar way, we can live with low integrity for only so long before some storm or shaking occurs and devastates the life we have constructed.

David pulled no punches and never tried to tiptoe around God. When he had a grievance, he expressed it; when he had done wrong, he laid his heart open, asking God to purify him. When he had a request, he asked with the respect of a king before the King. When he was in trouble or distress, he chose to praise the mightiness of his Lord and Savior rather than dwell on his threatening circumstances.

SOLOMON CAME TO KNOW HIS FATHER AS A MAN NOT WITHOUT FAULT OR SIN BUT A MAN OF GREAT INTEGRITY JUST THE SAME.

Truth and the ways of God mattered more to David than his own life. Solomon came to know his father as a man not without fault or sin but a man of great integrity just the same.

Because of David's passion for God, because of his faithfulness, righteousness, and uprightness of heart—his integrity—David's influence has lasted until this day. His psalms are treasured as some of the most pure worship songs ever written because of their honesty and boldness. The stories of David are some of the most retold stories of the Bible. We look to David for the courage he had before Goliath; we look to him for the faith and righteousness he had before Saul;

we look to his relationship with Jonathan as an example of true friendship. We see in David a man who sought to please God all the days of his life; we see in his repentance proof of God's willingness to forgive.

Can you, as Solomon aspired to do, follow David's example of passion, faithfulness, righteousness, and uprightness of heart to live with integrity? Are you steadfast in your daily life? Or are you distracted by circumstances, going days, weeks, or months without praying or praising God? Do you seek God's wisdom in all circumstances, or do you trust your own understanding when there are decisions to make?

Integrity has less to do with how things look on the outside than with our true internal strength. It has nothing to do with being perfect but everything to do with being honest—first with ourselves and then before others. *Integrity* means being willing to take responsibility for correcting errors whether we are really at fault or not. Jesus was the greatest example of this—though He never sinned, He spread His arms and accepted responsibility for the sin of all people and made salvation available to all.

When David failed, his first step was to restore fellowship with God, not organize a cover-up. The lesson he taught Solomon through the example of his own life is that integrity is not to be just one of our core values; it is to be our core. In his father, Solomon saw what it means to live with pure motives and proper priorities, staying focused on keeping our hearts right with God no matter what others think. Integrity is prizing fellowship with God above the admiration of others and letting nothing come between us and Him no matter what the cost.

A PRAYER FOR INTEGRITY

Father,

In the name of Jesus, I thank you for the examples of your Word. I thank you that because of Jesus I have an unshakable relationship with you and can know you even more fully than David and Solomon did.

Lord, I long to know you more fully. Teach me how to walk with you. Show me anything in my life that is keeping me from knowing you better, and show me how to deal with it. One of the highest acts of worship I can offer you is to be who you created me to be. Help me to be transparent, honest and real. Teach me to walk with integrity in all my ways.

Amen.

SOLOMON'S LIFE SECRET #3: LIVE WITH INTEGRITY

When God looks at you, does He see someone "after His own heart"?

Solomon recognized that God loved his father, David, because of David's faithfulness, righteousness, and uprightness of heart—his integrity. Although David sinned, he was always willing to repent. He sought God's righteousness, not his own.

God honored David and his son Solomon after him. So God will also bless you if you allow Him to instill the qualities of integrity in your life.

> *Search me, O God, and know my heart!*
> *Try me and know my thoughts!*
> *And see if there be any grievous way in me,*
> *and lead me in the way everlasting!*
> PSALM 139:23-24

Words to Live By

faithful
1: steadfast in affection or allegiance; loyal
2: firm in adherence to promises or in observance of duty

> *Your faithfulness endures to all generations;*
> *you have established the earth, and it stands fast.*
> Psalm 119: 90

repent
1: to turn from sin and dedicate oneself to the amendment of one's life
2a : to feel regret or contrition
 b : to change one's mind

> *Have mercy on me, O God, according to your steadfast love;*
> *. . . Wash me thoroughly from my iniquity, and cleanse me*
> *from my sin!* Psalm 51:1-2

integrity
1: firm adherence to a code of especially moral or artistic values ; incorruptibility
2: the quality or state of being complete or undivided

> *The righteous who walks in his integrity—*
> *blessed are his children after him!* Proverbs 20:7

·IV·
How to Be a Blessing

And you have kept for him this great and
steadfast love and have given him a son to sit
on his throne this day.

1 Kings 3:6

Riding his father's mule toward the springs at Gihon, Solomon could see the crowds there gathering water and wandering among the merchants' shops. Any public announcement made at Gihon traveled like water from the spring to every household in Jerusalem.

Solomon was nervous, despite his entourage of guards and servants. His older brother Adonijah was not far away at the southern spring of En-rogel, celebrating his self-appointment to the throne of Israel with nearly everyone in David's court except himself, Bathsheba, the prophet Nathan, Zadok the priest, and Benaiah son of Jehoiada, who all now took this journey with Solomon. David had commanded that Solomon be brought to Gihon to be anointed and announced as the next king of Israel. Either this would be the first step in establishing Solomon's rule, or it would plunge the nation into civil war.

Solomon slid off the mule and walked to the crest of the hill. The crowds seemed to have lost interest in gathering water and instead watched the royal procession with interest. With each step toward the knoll, Solomon felt the increasing weight of the people's expectations.

At the top of the hill, he knelt before Zadok, who held the horn of anointing oil and poured it out over Solomon's bowed head.

Trumpets sounded all around. "Long live King Solomon!" shouted the crowds. The people played flutes to express their joy as Solomon took a seat in a canopied chair, and the celebration began. Israel had reason for singing, dancing, and praise. Israel had a new king!

———————— ✒ ————————

Solomon had been blessed to be a blessing; his calling was clear. But just as God gave Solomon the name "beloved of

God" from his birth, knowing that one day Solomon would rule God's people, God also calls us in accord with His purpose and grace for the times in which we live.

God doesn't care how old you are, who's in your family, the color of your skin, whether you were born in the right part of town or even the right town. God will pass over millions to find someone whose heart is truly His. As Hanani said to King Asa of Judah:

> The eyes of the LORD run to and fro throughout the whole earth, to give strong support to those whose heart is blameless toward him.
> 2 CHRONICLES 16:9

And then once He has found such a heart, He will start building His kingdom—a little pocket of heaven on earth—around that person, for the blessing of all who come near.

YOUR PLACE IN THE KINGDOM

We often miss the simplicity of Jesus' message. As He began His ministry, Jesus expressed it in its entirety in one simple phrase: "The kingdom of heaven is at hand" (Matthew 3:2).

When Adam and Eve sinned, the human race was separated from God and God's will. Eden, with the tree of life at its center, could no longer be home. It was as if God had created a bubble of His perfect will around Adam and Eve, but their sin broke and lost that bubble. Jesus came to restore all that was lost. Those who are redeemed through His sacrifice don't relocate to Eden, of course, but in each of us a "bubble" of the kingdom of God forms—where the will of God can be done on earth as it is in heaven.

IN EACH OF US A "BUBBLE" OF THE KINGDOM OF GOD FORMS—WHERE THE WILL OF GOD CAN BE DONE ON EARTH AS IT IS IN HEAVEN.

"Wait a minute," you may say. "Isn't God sovereign? Can't He just make His will happen wherever He would like?"

God is indeed sovereign, but He will never impose His will on anyone. God already knew what Solomon would request in his dream, but He still showed up to give Solomon opportunity to ask. Solomon had to ask; then God would act.

While the kingdom Solomon sought to strengthen was a physical kingdom, the kingdom Jesus spoke of is spiritual, planted in our hearts by the Holy Spirit and nourished within us through the Word of God and prayer. The more of Him we get on the inside—the more of ourselves we surrender to make room for Him—the stronger His kingdom is within us. Growing in His light, spiritual fruit thrives:

"But the fruit of the Spirit is love, joy, peace, patience, kindness, goodness, faithfulness, gentleness, self-control" (Galatians 5:22-23). Soon we have more than we can enjoy ourselves, so the overflow begins to extend to others. When this happens, we touch our world in new and profound ways, and the kingdom of God begins to expand everywhere we go.

CHRISTIANS STAND BEFORE GOD ON BEHALF OF OUR WORLD, INTERCESSORS LIFTING UP HOLY HANDS ON BEHALF OF ALL PEOPLES OF THE EARTH.

Just as Israel stood before God as His chosen people in the time of Solomon, so the church stands before God as His chosen kingdom on earth today. Just as the priests of Solomon's day stood before God on behalf of the people, Christians stand before God on behalf of our world, intercessors lifting up holy hands on behalf of all peoples of the earth. Just as Solomon's responsibilities went beyond the simple care of his own household, so do ours. As Peter said:

> You are a chosen people, a royal priesthood, a holy nation, a people belonging to God, that you may declare the praises of him who called you out of darkness into his wonderful light.
> 1 PETER 2:9 NIV

Are you hungry to live more, get more out of life, fulfill the longing in your heart to make a difference? Finding your place in the kingdom of God is a secure place to begin.

CLUES TO YOUR CALLING

While all of us share responsibility to bear God's light to the world, each of us also has an individual calling, unique to who God created us to be and why. Clues to your calling are in your heart. Simply by paying attention to your desires, gifts, and talents, you can begin to understand the path and plan He has for your life.

Your desires are one of the first clues to your calling. David talks of this in Psalm 37:

> Trust in the LORD, and do good;
> dwell in the land and befriend faithfulness.
> Delight yourself in the LORD,
> and he will give you the desires of your heart.
> PSALM 37:3-4

Christians sometimes fear their desires because desires can become so easily corrupted. However, look at the protections David lists in this passage: trust in the Lord, do good, dwell in the land [in the place He has put you], befriend [pursue] faithfulness, delight yourself in the Lord. Do these things, and God will give you the desires of your heart. Your desires will be the proper ones for what He wants accomplished through you, and He will see that they are fulfilled.

Notice that these instructions have no prerequisites. You don't have to be a certain age, have experience or training, or go anywhere special—you can start following God's instructions and protecting your desires right now, right where you are. It's not necessary to say "when I finally find the right job ... when I find a spouse ... when I finish school ... when I get that next promotion—then I will think about spiritual things." No, anything you put ahead of God's instructions will only get in the way of God's plans and purposes for your life—and that is exactly how desires do get distorted. But if you pursue God in your quiet times and pursue living by His ways the rest of the time— that is when you can trust your heart's desires. That is the lifestyle that opens you to God's blessings.

> PURSUE GOD IN YOUR QUIET TIMES AND PURSUE LIVING BY HIS WAYS THE REST OF THE TIME— THAT IS WHEN YOU CAN TRUST YOUR HEART'S DESIRES.

So, what do you enjoy doing? What drives you crazy? What tugs at your heart when you see or hear about it? The desires God puts into your heart can be crucial to understanding the life He has in mind for you.

The gifts and talents God has placed in your life are a second clue to your calling. If God is calling you to follow a certain path, He will also equip you to be successful in it. This doesn't mean you won't have to work hard to develop your skills, but whatever comes naturally for you can indicate what God wants for your life. Are you a natural musician? Good with numbers? Great at working with children or helping people settle disputes? Are you a natural when it comes to art or decoration? Can you figure out how to fix almost anything, given the right tools? Are you athletic, inspirational, frugal, quick to catch on to new ideas, organized? All these gifts and many others can help you discover your purpose and calling.

An Ongoing Journey

Sometimes our hearts just seem to know that we are meant to follow a particular path, but more often than not, finding our purpose and path through life is an ongoing journey. From time to time we will spot mile markers and signposts, but the destination is not always spelled out up front.

In fact, it is really better that it isn't. Solomon's life shows us that such a great, clear start can give way to long-term failure. While in Solomon's prayer and his writings we find tremendous insight and wisdom, in his life we also find eventual failure because he lost touch with God. Turning from the counsel of God, Solomon married many foreign wives and eventually began to worship their gods. He grew self-sufficient and explored all the pleasures the world had to offer, and they left him empty, bitter, and depressed. Although he knew his calling early in life and was given great, godly wisdom to manage the daily affairs of the kingdom, his greatness faded. Solomon's son Rehoboam seems to have caught from Solomon only self-indulgence and conceit. When his counselors called for reform, Rehoboam chose instead to follow the advice of younger men full of selfish ambition and arrogance, and Israel's kingdom was divided. (See 1 Kings 12:1-24.)

For us the message is simple: begin in prayer, walk in prayer, and pray through to the end. When we don't know the end in every detail, the need for fresh guidance and the leadership of the Holy Spirit remains a priority. As Paul instructs in the book of Galatians: "Let us keep in step with the Spirit" (Galatians 5:25 NIV). How can we keep in step with Him if we don't pray and read His Word to seek His guidance?

IT'S NOT ABOUT YOU

One of the most interesting things about finding our purpose is that while it is intimately connected to our own sense of accomplishment and fulfillment, it is really more about the lives we touch than about obtaining a blessing for ourselves. And even the blessing we do receive may have much to do with connecting to others.

Solomon's concern—as we will explore in more detail in chapter six—was that now that he knew his calling to be king, a multitude of people needed him to do well as king in order for their lives to go well. Solomon's decisions would affect everyone in Israel. He had no more room for false humility than he did for pride. If he were at all shy about pursuing God with his whole heart, an entire kingdom of people might suffer for it.

> GOD'S PROVISIONS WILL ALWAYS FIT HIS PLANS AND PROMISES.

We need to get all that God has for us and be all that we can be. God knew what Solomon needed, because He had planned out what Solomon could be if he walked in God's ways as David had. Plugging into God's plan is key to receiving all God has for us. God's provisions will always fit His plans and promises. And it is very likely that there is someone out there depending on our success.

If you will take time to pray and seek God's direction concerning His purpose for you, then you will surely impact your world. God's purpose always includes blessing others, and that is one of your highest callings as a follower of Jesus Christ.

A Prayer for Fulfilling God's Call

Father,

I come to you in Jesus' name to thank you for the calling and destiny you have given me to touch my world and show forth the glory of your light. Help me to walk in that light. Give me a hunger for prayer, so that I can learn to dwell more in your presence at all times and hear your voice for every step of my day.

Lord, light my path with your Word. Show me the strengths you have put into me for your purposes as well as the weaknesses that I need to overcome. Meld my heart to those you have called me to work with to touch my world. Let the fruit of the Spirit grow in my life until it overflows to all around me.

I pray that your will be done on earth just as it is in heaven, and that you will guide me this day to be the blessing to others you want me to be. Give me insight and wisdom to know how to act as an example of your light and love to those you bring across my path.

Amen.

Solomon's Life Secret #4: Find your purpose

Each of us has a part in God's plan to extend His kingdom and bless the world. Finding out where you fit into His plan is crucial for your own fulfillment and so you can be a blessing to others. God will reveal your calling to you in due time if you are seeking Him in all your ways. Whether as a wealthy king or a missionary in an impoverished land, you will be successful. You will be exactly where God wants you, and He will equip you so that you won't fail. That is success!

Are you open to whatever the Lord might be telling you to do? Are you willing to let go of whatever dream you may have for yourself and accept the plan and purpose God has for you?

> *Many are the plans in the mind of a man,*
> *but it is the purpose of the LORD that will stand. . . .*
> *The purpose in a man's heart is like deep water,*
> *but a man of understanding will draw it out.*
> Proverbs 19:21; 20:5

WORDS TO LIVE BY

calling
1: a strong inner impulse toward a particular course of
   action especially when accompanied by conviction
   of divine influence

> [God] saved us and called us to a holy calling, not because of
> our works but because of his own purpose and grace, which he
> gave us in Christ Jesus before the ages began. 2 TIMOTHY 1:9

purpose
1a : something set up as an object or end to be attained;
     intention
  b : resolution, determination

> In him we have obtained an inheritance, having been predes-
> tined according to the purpose of him who works all things
> according to the counsel of his will. EPHESIANS 1:11

influence
1: an emanation of spiritual or moral force
2: the act or power of producing an effect without apparent
   exertion of force or direct exercise of command

> By the blessing of the influence of the upright and God's favor
> [because of them] the city is exalted. PROVERBS 11:11 AMP

·V·

†rue Greatness

*And now, O LORD my God, you have made your
servant king in place of David my father, although
I am but a little child. I do not know how to go out or
come in.*

1 Kings 3:7

In the days that followed Solomon's anointing, Solomon
followed his father David's instructions to the letter.
Men who had betrayed his father were executed or exiled.
When Adonijah asked to marry David's last concubine,
echoing Absalom's traitorous act of sleeping with his
father's harem in a tent on the palace roof, Solomon had
Adonijah executed as a traitor as well. Harsh decisions for
harsh times, but all according to the political wisdom his
father had provided from his deathbed.

All of his life Solomon had looked to his father for wisdom; what was he to do now that David was gone? David had left Solomon no other instructions except the example of his own life and the word that had been given to David about his inheritance from the Lord:

> If your sons pay close attention to their way, to walk before me in faithfulness with all their heart and with all their soul, you shall not lack a man on the throne of Israel.
> 1 Kings 2:4

It appeared Solomon had a choice: either he had to find someone else to look to as he once had his father or he had to form the kind of relationship with God his father had.

Solomon knew what to do. It was time for a retreat. He ordered preparations for a trip to Gibeon, where he would make a thousand sacrifices to the Lord and then wait upon Him in prayer and worship. This was God's kingdom, after all, not his. If God wanted him to rule it correctly, then Solomon knew he had to get a word from God to know how to proceed, and he also knew that God would not fail him in this. At least that much he had learned from his father.

To receive anything from anyone, we must first acknowledge that he or she has something that we want or need. Think about the relationship between students and teachers. Students must see themselves as vessels ready to be filled with information and instruction, acknowledging their dependence on their teachers in order to learn. To receive, students must approach their classes from a position of humility—understanding that there is something valuable in their teachers that they need to receive.

It is the same, as Solomon recognized, when we want to receive from God.

AN ATTITUDE OF HUMILITY

Pride blinds us to our need. There is nothing more intoxicating than pride, and though it hardly ever causes a noticeable hangover, it is much more difficult to sober up from. It distorts our view of the world, lowers our inhibitions, and warps our consciences. It makes us think we are self-sufficient and causes us to align with those who agree with us and to spurn those who challenge us. Prideful leaders, seeking only to build their own "palaces" and forgetting to raise the overall standards of their "kingdoms," fill their advisory boards with yes people and look for admiration rather than accomplishment.

Pride can also be the root cause when we find ourselves sitting in judgment of others. "Judging" is definitely the right word to describe this little exercise because just as a judge sits above the courtroom dealing out sentences and punishment to the people below him, we place ourselves above others when we judge them. We deceptively see ourselves in a lofty position and feel justified in our assessment of others' shortcomings, thinking we are better because the particular vice we are judging holds no temptation for us. But we fail to see the "planks" in our own eyes in other areas. (See Matthew 7:1-5 NIV.)

TRUE HUMILITY COMES FROM KNOWING OUR POSITION IN RELATIONSHIP TO A LOVING GOD.

The only cure for this "judgment disease" is true humility. That is when we see ourselves accurately from God's perspective, freely admitting that we all fall short of God's perfection, and see our need for forgiveness. We begin to realize that every person on this planet is in the same boat; no one is better than another. We discover that the ground at the cross is really level.

As we admit our own failures and weaknesses and at the same time acknowledge and accept God's remedy—Jesus' sacrifice—we are exercising the opposite of pride, which is humility. True humility comes from knowing our position in relationship to a loving God.

However, sometimes in the exercise of humility we still can miss it. At one extreme, people are sometimes "humble" to the point of taking pride in how humble they are! Others lack any backbone to stand up for themselves and could use some assertiveness training. They let the world happen to them and never make much of a difference to anyone. Others equate being humble with making themselves doormats to others. This is a gross misunderstanding of the term. While there is an element of submission and preferring others before ourselves, humility is not a place of powerlessness but a place of knowing who we are—both on our own and in Christ—and what our true authority is.

> SOME PEOPLE MISTAKE HUMILITY FOR LOWLINESS, WHEN HUMILITY IS REALLY A MATTER OF GRATITUDE FOR WHAT OTHERS HAVE TO OFFER

The great missionary, minister, and author Andrew Murray wrote, "There are three great motivations to humility: it becomes us as creatures; it becomes us as sinners; and it becomes us as saints." In other words, humility is an appropriate attitude for us because we are beings created by God, because we make mistakes, but also because we are blessed by grace to redemption. Far too often, Christians emphasize only the second reason for humility in Murray's list—that we are sinners—not realizing that humility is more a product of the grace we have received than the mistakes of our past or the weaknesses of the present.

Some people mistake humility for lowliness, when humility is really a matter of gratitude for what others have to offer, rather than an attitude of groveling. Humble people can be honest about their strengths and weaknesses; they can work with others as both a teammate and a team leader at the same time. Humility understands guilt and grace, love and justice, ability and need. Having humility can seem a delicate balance, but living in that balance is an important skill we all need to master. Humility is living with an attitude perhaps best summed up by Paul in his letter to the Romans:

> By the grace given to me I say to everyone among you not to think of himself more highly than he ought to think, but to think with sober judgment, each according to the measure of faith that God has assigned.
> ROMANS 12:3

This description of humility is echoed in Scripture by the only two people Jesus commended as having great faith.

Humility and Faith

The first person commended for faith by Jesus was a Roman centurion who asked Jesus to heal his servant. The centurion's humility and faith were drawn from his understanding of authority. He said to Jesus:

> "Lord, I am not worthy to have you come under my roof, but only say the word, and my servant will be healed. For I too am a man under authority, with soldiers under me. And I say to one, 'Go,' and he goes, and to another, 'Come,' and he comes, and to my servant, 'Do this,' and he does it." When Jesus heard this, he marveled and said to those who followed him, "Truly, I tell you, with no one in Israel have I found such faith."
> Matthew 8:8-10

There is no question that this centurion was a humble man. His attitude toward Jesus was that he, a Gentile, was not fit to have Jesus in his home. He was not demeaning himself; he was honoring Jesus. He also cared enough about his servant, a person far below himself in rank, to ask for the servant's healing. He saw a situation beyond his authority—the sickness of his servant—and knew he needed help.

This centurion was the commander of a hundred men in a great army. His authority was backed by an empire. He was far from powerless; the finest doctors in the land would have been available to him. When he gave an order, people moved quickly to obey. Why would such a man come to Jesus with respect and deference? Why didn't he just order Jesus to heal his servant?

The centurion did indeed have great authority, but he knew his authority came from Caesar and Jesus' authority came from heaven. In comparison, Caesar's power was insignificant. So it was that this officer came humbly before Jesus—helmet in hand, if you will—and made his request in absolute faith that simply by Jesus' word his servant would be healed. Humbly he came; humbly he received.

The centurion's humility did not come from thinking he was nothing but from knowing just where he fit in the chain of authority in the universe. He did not think higher of himself than he ought, but neither did he think less of himself than was necessary. His authority let him know that he had an obligation of respect for and submission to those above him and responsibility for those under his command. True humility expresses itself by taking compassionate responsibility for those below you in God's chain of command and being joyfully obedient to those who have authority over you.

This is why meekness—which is akin to humility—is

included as a fruit of the Spirit in the list in Galatians 5: 22-23. Meekness is the refusal to exalt oneself over another. We can be meek only when we have absolute confidence that God is our defender. Meekness requires complete trust that God sees us and rewards us according to His Word. When we are meek, we can leave promotion and success in God's hands and not strive to manipulate situations for our own benefit. This is often a longer road than self-promotion, but in the end far more rewarding.

The Bible tells us that God considered Moses to be the meekest person of all the people on the earth. (See Numbers 12:3.) Why? Because whenever Moses was defied or challenged, he fell to his face and called out to God for what to do. When God did show up, those who had questioned Moses' authority were always sorry they had dared to speak against God's chosen leader.

The second person Jesus commended for great faith was a woman who asked Jesus to heal her daughter:

> Jesus . . . withdrew to the district of Tyre and Sidon. And behold, a Canaanite woman from that region came out and was crying, "Have mercy on me, O Lord, Son of David; my daughter is severely oppressed by a demon." But he did not answer her a word. And his disciples came and begged him,

saying, "Send her away, for she is crying out after us." He answered, "I was sent only to the lost sheep of the house of Israel." But she came and knelt before him, saying, "Lord, help me." And he answered, "It is not right to take the children's bread and throw it to the dogs." She said, "Yes, Lord, yet even the dogs eat the crumbs that fall from their masters' table." Then Jesus answered her, "O woman, great is your faith! Be it done for you as you desire." And her daughter was healed instantly.

MATTHEW 15:21-28

Here is a remarkable story on so many levels. Look at this woman's faith and tenacity! A non-Jew, she knew she had no right to expect anything from Jesus; He had not come to help her people. When Jesus called her people dogs, she accepted the comment as justified; she knew where she stood in the world at that time. But even more she knew the love of God and her own love for her daughter. Her response to Jesus was impetuous and could even be construed as insubordinate, yet from her place of humility this woman knew that no was not really the answer God wanted to give her. She knew to bow her head, make her request, and stay until heaven broke through on her behalf, no matter what the circumstances looked

TRUE HUMILITY IS NOT POSSIBLE WITHOUT GREAT FAITH IN GOD'S PROMISES.

like, how she was treated, or who others thought she was. True humility is not possible without great faith in God's promises.

Humility and Heaven

Solomon was king—not a position we normally associate with humility. But Solomon knew his authority was God-given, his favor with God an inheritance from his father, and his responsibility to people God had called him to lead. So, when God appeared to him in his dream, Solomon responded with grateful words focused on God's goodness and lovingkindness. Solomon acknowledged that his gifts and position were no reason for pride, but instead a reason to be grateful. Though arguably the greatest man in Israel, Solomon chose to bow his knee before God so that he could be the servant of all. Instead of asking God for his own greatness, he requested wisdom so that God's people could be a great nation—and for the forty years of Solomon's reign, they were.

Suppose a child receives a special gift from his parents for his birthday—something every other child wants. He can share it or stow it away in the back of his closet, never letting anyone else play with it. It all depends on the nature of the gift—and the child—but it is his to do with as he would like. Why was the gift given? Simply because Mom and Dad love the child. If the child begins to feel special because of the gift, however, and starts holding himself above his friends and bossing them around, that would be out of place. If he is to feel special at all, it should be because of his parents' love, not because of their gift. Children are not always mature thinkers, however.

Neither are adults. Too often we fall into the trap of believing we are something special because of what we have been given, forgetting the One who gave us the gifts. Instead of falling into pride because of our gifts, we should, like Solomon, exercise humility and be grateful for the love those gifts express. God needs humble kings, not proud paupers.

And one of the best ways to express gratitude for our gifts is to use them as God intended and see that they are a blessing to as many people as possible. As Solomon himself said,

> The reward for humility and fear of the LORD
> is riches and honor and life.
> PROVERBS 22:4

Humility is the only place we have to stand to receive from

God and to share His blessings with others. Humility is the only basis for the blessing of the Lord that makes a person rich but "adds no sorrow with it" (Proverbs 10:22).

While some have accomplished great things without being humble, truly great human beings are always humble. Humility is the foundation for all righteous leadership and nobility. Solomon was humble; he asked to be a blessing rather than to be personally blessed. We can learn from Solomon's humility and adopt his attitude to touch our world as God has called us to do in our time.

A Prayer for Humility

Father,

In Jesus' name, thank you that you have called me to be a child and an heir in your kingdom. You have put me in the place where I am to make a difference for your kingdom by shining forth the light of your love.

Lord, give me a teachable spirit and teach me the bold humility of the centurion and the Canaanite woman. I want to trust completely in your Word alone and have the tenacity never to let go of your promises or lose confidence in your goodness and love. Keep me from pride and give me the humility to know that my best hope for the future starts anew every day, praying for your wisdom and guidance for every step. Lead me by your Spirit of wisdom and truth.

I trust in you always. Guide me and teach me your ways. Amen.

Solomon's Life Secret #5:
Be humble

Solomon chose to humble himself like a child before God, and God was able to make him great. We exercise humility when we understand our relationship to a loving God and trust Him in faith to care for us as He has promised. True humility requires great faith. How humble are you, and how strong is your faith?

> *When pride comes, then comes disgrace,*
> *but with the humble is wisdom.*
> Proverbs 11:2

WORDS TO LIVE BY

humble

1: not proud or haughty; not arrogant or assertive
2: reflecting, expressing, or offered in a spirit of deference or submission, <a humble apology>

> *Pride lands you flat on your face;*
> *humility prepares you for honors.* PROVERBS 29:23 THE
> MESSAGE

gift

1: a notable capacity, talent, or endowment
2: something voluntarily transferred by one person to another without compensation

> *So we, though many, are one body in Christ, and individually*
> *members one of another. Having gifts that differ according to*
> *the grace given to us, let us use them.* ROMANS 12:5-6

·VI·
THE HEART OF A SERVANT

Your servant is in the midst of your people whom you
have chosen, a great people, too many to be numbered or
counted for multitude.

1 KINGS 3:8

Solomon stood on the balcony of David's palace looking out over Mount Zion. In the four years since he had become king, Israel had risen for the first time to be master of all she surveyed. Through marriage, Egypt was an ally; the nations of the Promised Land before the Israelites arrived had all been destroyed or now paid Solomon tribute. The kingdom of Israel now bordered Phoenicia and the Euphrates in the north, Egypt in the south, the Mediterranean and Philistia in the west, and the Aramean desert to the east.

Israel was now the greatest nation on earth and Solomon

the greatest king. Many advised him that it was time to enjoy life—build a new and grander palace, expand the walls of Jerusalem, extend the treasuries.

But Solomon's priorities were different.

God's dwelling place in Israel was still a tent. His people had a permanent home; the land they had entered as foreigners now belonged to them. Wasn't it time for their God to have a permanent dwelling place as well, just as his father, David, had always wanted to build?

"Your highness, the servants of Hiram, king of Tyre, have arrived and requested an audience."

Solomon did not turn. "Let them enter."

Hiram's servants knelt before Solomon in honor and praised his work. "King Hiram sends his greetings to his friend's son—for King Hiram always loved your father, David—and pledges Tyre's continued friendship with Israel. This tribute is but a token. Whatever Tyre can do for the house of Solomon, you have but to ask."

Solomon smiled. He remembered Hiram from his youth. He was a good friend to his father indeed, and Tyre provided the best wood for building from the Mediterranean to the eastern deserts. If Solomon was to build a temple for the Lord, surely Hiram was the first person he should ask for help.

Solomon turned at last to Hiram's servants. "I have a message for you to take to King Hiram."

> You know that David my father could not build a house for the name of the LORD his God because of the warfare with which his enemies surrounded him, until the LORD put them under the soles of his feet. But now the LORD my God has given me rest on every side. There is neither adversary nor misfortune. And so I intend to build a house for the name of the LORD my God, as the LORD said to David my father, "Your son, whom I will set on your throne in your place, shall build the house for my name." Now therefore command that cedars of Lebanon be cut for me. And my servants will join your servants, and I will pay you for your servants such wages as you set, for you know that there is no one among us who knows how to cut timber like the Sidonians.
>
> 1 KING 5:3-6.

Solomon continued gazing at Mount Zion after Hiram's servants had departed. He would wait for Hiram's reply, and when he received it, he would command that the work to build a temple on Mount Zion for the Lord should commence immediately. Before he built a palace of his own, Solomon would ensure that his father's dream of a permanent dwelling place on earth for the Lord would be accomplished.

The Bible tells us that "as soon as Hiram heard the words of Solomon, he rejoiced greatly and said, 'Blessed be the Lord this day, who has given to David a wise son to be over this great people'"(1 Kings 5:7). Hiram recognized Solomon's wisdom and his servant heart.

CHOOSING TO SERVE

In the Bible, there are two kinds of servants, slaves and bondservants, although the terms are sometimes used interchangeably. Slaves, owned by their masters, were taken against their will or sold by their families to pay off a debt. Joseph was this kind of slave in Egypt, as were all the Israelites under Pharaoh when Moses was sent to deliver them. It's easy to imagine that many slaves looked forward to the day of their release and worked as little as they could get away with. If a slave saw a possibility of escape, he often took it.

Bondservants, however, worked off their debt but then chose to remain in their master's service, desiring to please their master and be a blessing in every way possible. A bondservant never looked just to get the job done but worked with an attitude that made him stand out. Although he was Potiphar's slave in Egypt, Joseph was a good example of the attitude of a bondservant. His work was so excellent and his attitude so trustworthy that Potiphar confidently put him in charge of running his entire estate.

"Servant leaders" today are those who desire to be a blessing to everyone who crosses their path and every project or assignment they touch. Servant leaders choose to work for the benefit of the team they supervise (or the family they support). They build others up so that all can advance together. They can be trusted.

SERVANT LEADERS ... BUILD OTHERS UP SO THAT ALL CAN ADVANCE TOGETHER.

They reflect this admonition in Paul's letter to the church at Ephesus:

> Slaves, obey your earthly masters with fear and trembling, with a sincere heart, as you would Christ, not by the way of eye-service, as people-pleasers, but as servants of Christ, doing the will of God from the heart, rendering service with a good will as to the Lord and not to man, knowing that whatever good anyone does, this he will receive back from the Lord, whether he is a slave or free.
> EPHESIANS 6:5-8

Solomon was this kind of servant leader. He looked at God's people as a great nation to be served, not tools for building his personal empire and fame. He was their king for their benefit, not his own. As such a leader, he chose to do what he could to bless his entire nation and his God before he saw to his own desires. So it was that he built the temple as the first project of his rule and spared no expense to construct it of the finest materials, handled by the best craftsmen. Building God a permanent dwelling place in Jerusalem would be the ultimate step in securing the future of God's people, a symbol and a place of prayer to the Lord continually.

CHOOSING RESPONSIBILITY

Another mark of a true servant is looking for responsibility rather than seeking to avoid it. Though building the temple had been his father's dream, Solomon took on the responsibility of accomplishing the task. He also willingly accepted the responsibility of guiding his people and judging fairly in their disputes.

Of course, the ultimate example of willingly choosing responsibility is Jesus. He never sinned, yet He accepted the penalty for an entire world of sin when He stretched out His arms on the cross.

Another mark of a servant heart is intercessory prayer. Are you willing to stand in the gap to help others you may not even know? Are you willing to pray as Paul instructed so that your community might experience the light and goodness of Christ?

> I urge that supplications, prayers, intercessions, and thanks-
> givings be made for all people, for kings and all who are in
> high positions, that we may lead a peaceful and quiet life,
> godly and dignified in every way. This is good, and it is pleas-
> ing in the sight of God our Savior, who desires all people to be
> saved and to come to the knowledge of the truth.
> 1 Timothy 2:1-4

Servants who choose responsibility are willing to pray for the governments of all nations and for churches besides their own. The world needs intercessors to pray for other believers who need God's promises fulfilled or are experiencing persecution somewhere else in the world. Are you willing to lift up holy hands in prayer for others before you lay your own requests at the foot of God's throne in heaven?

The Importance of Obedience

We tend to think that greatness means exercising power over others. Proverbs 30:21-22 warns that a slave who becomes king will be a tyrant. Yet a bondservant obeys someone else in all things.

In the book of Matthew, Jesus spoke with His disciples

about greatness in the kingdom of heaven.

> At that time the disciples came to Jesus, saying, "Who is the
> greatest in the kingdom of heaven?" And calling to him a
> child, he put him in the midst of them and said, "Truly, I say
> to you, unless you turn and become like children, you will
> never enter the kingdom of heaven. Whoever humbles himself
> like this child is the greatest in the kingdom of heaven."
> MATTHEW 18:1-4

The disciples were struggling for position and authority within the physical kingdom they thought Jesus would one day establish. Perhaps trying to hide their intent, they phrased their question in spiritual terms: "Who is the greatest in the kingdom of heaven?"

Jesus' response was twofold. He called to a young child, maybe a child running by, and the child came and stood in the midst of the disciples. An attitude of childlikeness, Jesus said, is necessary to enter the kingdom of heaven. What attributes define childlikeness? Innocence, curiosity, joy, and especially simple faith and willingness to trust.

But Jesus had a second point. We can imagine Him continuing, "You want to be great? You will need to be humble like this child, then." As we saw in chapter five, humility has to do with gratitude and with understanding our relationship to God and our place in His plans. The humility of a child causes him to trust in those who provide for him; he knows he is dependent on them. This is the usual explanation of the lesson of this passage of Scripture: true greatness in the kingdom of heaven requires a childlike trust. Yet could there be another layer to Jesus' explanation? Isn't greatness in the kingdom of God also tied to obedience?

Scripture gives no indication that the child Jesus called and stood among the disciples was anyone special. It wasn't Paul as a boy or someone who grew up to be a leading church father. This was just a child who stopped whatever he or she was doing when Jesus called and did what He asked. Maybe this child didn't want to stop his play. Maybe he was on an urgent errand for his parent—perhaps someone was sick and the child was going to get the doctor, or maybe he was going to the market to buy dinner. Yet, whatever the child was doing, when Jesus called the child simply stopped and obeyed Jesus' request.

Jesus' keys to greatness then? To be the servant of all and to trust and obey as a little child.

SELF-CONTROL AND TRUE FREEDOM

No situation or person can make us a slave if we choose

instead to be a servant. Faced with a dead-end job, a physical handicap, or a dysfunctional family—we have a choice to make. We can choose to be ruled by the situation, or we can choose to grow in it and be a blessing.

Look again at Joseph. His brothers, fed up with their father's favoritism and Joseph's own youthful ego, decide to sell him into slavery in Egypt. This is a one-way, dead-end street for Joseph. However, once in Egypt, rather than complain and surrender to his lot in life, he chooses instead to trust God and serve with all his heart. As a result his master, Potiphar, begins to prosper, and then so does Joseph—he is placed over all of his master's affairs.

> NO SITUATION OR PERSON CAN MAKE US A SLAVE IF WE CHOOSE INSTEAD TO BE A SERVANT.

Then Potiphar's wife notices Joseph and wants him to sleep with her, but Joseph refuses to sin against his master and against God that way. Spurned, Potiphar's wife accuses Joseph of attempted rape, and he is imprisoned with no trial. If things looked bad when he was first sent to Egypt, they looked much worse now; Egyptian jails were not known for their hospitable accommodations.

But again, instead of complaining, Joseph chooses to serve, and so he is blessed and ends up running the place just as he did Potiphar's household. In the midst of the worst of situations, he continues to hone his gifts. Then, desperate to understand a dream, Pharaoh calls on Joseph, and Joseph is ready and able to handle the opportunity. In one day, he goes from the gutter to the executive suite and never looks back.

One of the reasons for Joseph's success is that he chose to serve and refused to be a slave—not only to circumstances but also to his own passions. Had he given in to Potiphar's wife, he would not have met Pharaoh's baker in jail, and he would have missed his appointment with destiny.

Although self-control is last in the list of spiritual fruit in Galatians 5:22-23, it also feeds all the others. Without self-control to choose what is right—to choose to follow God's Word and the leading of the Holy Spirit—love, joy, peace, patience, kindness, goodness, faithfulness, and gentleness can't grow freely in our lives. Jesus said that we are slaves to sin until He sets us free. (See John 8:34-36.) Only those who choose to serve the Father—as Joseph did and as Jesus did—will ever be truly free; others will always be in bondage to their passions and circumstances.

Solomon chose to serve God at the beginning of his reign, but in his later years he chose differently, and the negative impact on his life and influence was significant. If you want to have the heart of a servant, then you will need to develop the spiritual muscle to choose to serve no matter what the circumstances. And sometimes our ability to do this is hindered by our low "trust factor." What is the trust factor? It is our ability to decide, in the face of overwhelming odds, to believe that God really is on our side—that He wants to and will take care of us and our personal interests.

ONLY THOSE WHO CHOOSE TO SERVE THE FATHER—AS JOSEPH DID AND AS JESUS DID—WILL EVER BE TRULY FREE; OTHERS WILL ALWAYS BE IN BONDAGE TO THEIR PASSIONS AND CIRCUMSTANCES.

This is really our great dilemma. On the one hand, we feel compassion for others and are stirred from within to use our gifts and resources to serve them. But, on the other hand, when we feel threatened or fearful that our own needs will not be met, we have the natural tendency to slip back into the shell of "look out for number one." We suffer from a hidden suspicion of God. *Does He really care? Does He really have my best interest at heart?* we ask ourselves. This kind of thinking only leads to our taking matters into our own hands and, as a result, we turn our focus from others to ourselves.

So, what is the answer? When we are tempted by these

thoughts, we must remember that Jesus gave up all His rights and privileges, at great personal cost, for our sakes. He understands the meaning of sacrifice—He lived it! Yet He did it willingly because of the great love He has for us. If that doesn't forever settle the question of whether or not He cares, what would? His actions definitely proved the affirmative. Why not ask the Lord to seal the fact of His unfailing love and care for you in your heart so that you can truly live with a servant's heart?

A Prayer for a Servant's Heart

Father,

In the name of Jesus, I praise and thank you for the great sacrifice you made on my behalf. Help me to know that your sacrifice proves that you will always care for me, that you will never leave me defenseless.

Help me now to serve you with an obedient heart and to serve others with all of the resources you have blessed me with.

Help me to know your Word and obey it, trusting you and knowing that when I submit you are quick to defend me from harm.

Guide my steps, Father, that I may walk in all that you have called me to, and check my heart that my attitude would always glorify you. Let your light shine through me everywhere I go.

Amen.

Solomon's Life Secret #6: Choose to serve and obey

Solomon reigned with a servant's heart, using his authority to be a blessing to generations. A true servant humbles himself and seeks what is best for others because he knows that God will look after his own interests. And, like Solomon, a true servant obeys the authority above him with a willing attitude. Like Solomon, you can become a blessing to those above you and those you are responsible for, if you choose to live with the heart of a servant.

What motivates you as you interact with others?

> *Care for the flock of God entrusted to you. Watch over it willingly, not grudgingly—not for what you will get out of it, but because you are eager to serve God. Don't lord it over the people assigned to your care, but lead them by your good example.*
> 1 Peter 5:2-3 NLT

WORDS TO LIVE BY

serve

1a : to be of use
 b : to be worthy of reliance or trust <if memory serves>

> *Whoever would be great among you must be your servant,*
> *and whoever would be first among you must be slave of all.*
> *For even the Son of Man came not to be served but to serve,*
> *and to give his life as a ransom for many.* MARK 10:43-45

responsible

1a : liable to be called on to answer
 b : liable to be called to account as the primary cause,
     motive, or agent
2 : able to answer for one's conduct and obligations, trust-
    worthy

> *Surely he has borne our griefs and carried our sorrows; . . .*
> *He was wounded for our transgressions;*
> *he was crushed for our iniquities;*
> *upon him was the chastisement that brought us peace,*
> *and with his stripes we are healed.* ISAIAH 53:4-5

VII

An Understanding Mind

> *Give your servant therefore an understanding mind to govern your people, that I may discern between good and evil, for who is able to govern this your great people?*
>
> 1 Kings 3:9

The women were prostitutes. What were they doing here? Solomon could see the disdain on the faces of those in his court as the two women came forward with a baby. According to the law of Moses, the women could be stoned to death, but here they were walking into the very court that could condemn them. What was so desperately important that they needed Solomon to decide for them? Why could the lower court not reach a decision?

The first woman began her testimony: "Oh, my lord, this woman and I live in the same house, and I gave birth to a child while she was in the house. Then on the third day after I gave birth, this woman also gave birth. And we were alone. There was no one else with us in the house; only we two were in the house. And this woman's son died in the night, because she lay on him. And she arose at midnight and took my son from beside me, while your servant slept, and laid him at her breast, and laid her dead son at my breast. When I rose in the morning to nurse my child, behold, he was dead. But when I looked at him closely in the morning, behold, he was not the child that I had borne."

The other woman interrupted. "No, the living child is mine, and the dead child is hers."

At this the two women fell to squabbling, and the child awoke and began to cry. Solomon gestured to his guards, who stepped in to separate the women. He looked at the child, and he wondered for a moment at God's design for family and the instinctual love of a mother for her child. Clearly this child deserved the love of its natural mother, but neither woman in this instance seemed reasonable or righteous.

The glossy veneer of shame hung over both women, yet as Solomon considered these things, he knew that if there was anything pure in either one, it would be that of a mother's love. To find it, he would have to judge with the harshness these women were used to, not the tenderness he preferred.

The throne room quieted again. Solomon looked at the two women without the slightest hint of compassion in his eyes and then turned to the gallery. "The one says, 'This is my son that is alive, and your son is dead'; and the other says, 'No; but your son is dead, and my son is the living one.'" He let the words settle, and then he turned to one of the guards. "Bring me a sword."

The soldier crossed to the king, unsheathing his sword. But Solomon did not reach to take it. "Divide the living child in two, and give half to the one and half to the other."

The guard turned toward the women and the child, sword at the ready.

"Oh, my lord!" pleaded the woman who had testified first. "Give her the living child, and by no means put him to death."

But the other woman shrieked, "He shall be neither mine nor yours; divide him!"

Solomon raised his hand to the guard, who halted. Through a callous exterior, the true mother's love had revealed itself in its mercy. Solomon then spoke for all to hear, "Give the living child to the first woman, and by no means put him to death; she is his mother."

He sat back on his throne. Conversation rippled through the room and eventually throughout all Israel, as people marveled at the wisdom of their king. No other judge in Israel had been able to discern the truth in this matter, but Solomon had done it.

We make hundreds of decisions every day, from what time to get up to how to manage our money, from how to respond to a supervisor's question to what the kids will do after school. Take that risk, or leave it? Let that person make the decision, or object because we disagree? Keep careful track of our priorities, or just do what keeps the peace? The ramifications of our choices will impact our lives that moment, the next day, or decades later. How can we, like Solomon, always make the right decision?

The answer is simple, although the application can be complex. The key to making the right decision is wisdom.

A TREE OF LIFE

Solomon dedicated much of the book of Proverbs to the importance of actively seeking wisdom in everything we do.

The benefits of having wisdom are immense:

> *Blessed is the one who finds wisdom,*
> *and the one who gets understanding,*
> *for the gain from her is better than gain from silver*
> *and her profit better than gold.*
> *She is more precious than jewels,*
> *and nothing you desire can compare with her.*
> *Long life is in her right hand;*
> *in her left hand are riches and honor.*
> *Her ways are ways of pleasantness,*
> *and all her paths are peace.*
> *She is a tree of life to those who lay hold of her;*
> *those who hold her fast are called blessed.*
> Proverbs 3:13-18

Riches can come and go, but the wise person will always bounce back from any adversity—as well as prosper in times of stability and peace. In wisdom's right hand (the favored hand in most traditions) is health and long life, while in her left hand is wealth and honor. All of her ways are pleasant and full of peace. *Wisdom*—the ability to make the right decision or to correctly apply the information at hand—is a tree of life that should never be left unnurtured!

Two Kinds of Wisdom

In 1 Corinthians 3:19, Paul tells us that "the wisdom of this world is foolishness to God" (NLT). What does the world consider wise? Dressing to impress, climbing the corporate ladder at work and the social ladder at home, acquiring all the latest electronic gadgets and gizmos, driving the latest model car, living in a trendy part of town, funding our retirement plans to the max, going into debt for what we can't afford, and depending on ourselves to pull all this off. Worldly wisdom says the right thing to do is to focus all the time on ourselves and our own needs and wants. It puts us in control and leaves God and His ways out of the equation.

However, we were not created to live according to worldly wisdom: "For everything in the world—the cravings of sinful man, the lust of his eyes and the boasting of what he has and does—comes not from the Father but from the world" (1 John 2:16 NIV). James tells us that such "wisdom" is from the devil. (James 3:15.)

The opposite of worldly wisdom is godly wisdom, which is understanding and living according to the principles God established. His principles make life work the way He intended. In the book of Proverbs, Solomon has much to say about the importance and impact of godly wisdom. He compares the lifestyle of the "fool" or the "wicked," those who reject or ignore God and His ways, and the wise, those who listen to what God has to say and live their lives in tune with Him. Among other traits, the fool is always after instant gratification, is lazy and undisciplined, lacks judgment, can't keep a confidence, won't learn from criticism, and thinks he is something special when he really is not! On the other hand, the wise person is disciplined, diligent, obedient, able to control his speech, humble, and willing to learn from others.

"Wisdom is more precious than rubies," Solomon tells us, "and nothing you desire can compare with her" (Proverbs 8:11 NIV). When we follow Solomon's advice and "get wisdom" (Proverbs 4:5), we find life the way God intended for us to experience it. "Blessed is the man who listens to me," wisdom tells us, "watching daily at my doors, waiting at my doorway. For whoever finds me finds life" (Proverbs 8:34-35 NIV).

> WHEN WE FOLLOW SOLOMON'S ADVICE AND "GET WISDOM," WE FIND LIFE THE WAY GOD INTENDED FOR US TO EXPERIENCE IT.

As we live with godly wisdom, our lives improve; we see the effects of wisdom in our lives and pursue God's ways even more. We become discerning. *Discernment* is the ability to see clearly what is right and what is wrong, what is true and what is false, what is important and what is insignificant, what squares with God's Word and what does not. It is the ability to see beyond the surface to the significant and beyond the natural and immediate to the spiritual and eternal. Solomon demonstrated discernment when he dealt with the two women arguing over which of them was actually the mother of the child they brought to him.

Discernment is the ability to find a path in the forest that others miss and a way through circumstances that could easily overwhelm. Discernment gives us the ability to size up a situation and not only avoid calamity but maximize benefit. A discerning person will know the right thing to do at the right time and in the right place. Those with discernment are cautious and able to avoid undesirable situations while others walk on blindly, or as Solomon put it:

> *The prudent sees danger and hides himself,*
> *but the simple go on and suffer for it.*
> PROVERBS 22:3

When God sent the angel Gabriel to Zechariah the priest before John the Baptist was born, the angel called godly wisdom "the wisdom of the righteous" (Luke 1:17 NIV). Who are the righteous? Those who completely place their trust in

Jesus Christ. Clearly, then, as followers of Jesus, we have a choice to make—will we conduct our lives according to the wisdom of the world around us or according to the wisdom of God? And how do we get godly wisdom? What values or priorities do we need in order to always act wisely? The book of Proverbs tells that us the most prominent keys to wisdom—and perhaps the most misunderstood—are the fear of the Lord plus instruction and discipline.

THE FEAR OF THE LORD

Solomon called the fear of the Lord the beginning of wisdom. (See Proverbs 9:10.) Many believe that to know much is to be wise. Knowledge, however, is simply factual information. Both the wise and the foolish can have knowledge—what differentiates them is how they use it.

The fool (someone who disregards God) will use knowledge to benefit himself despite what is right or ethical, because the fool believes there is no greater good in the universe than his own benefit. The wise person, however, knows there is no greater good than pleasing God and uses knowledge in a different way—respecting God and following His ways. Fear of the Lord—respecting God and following His ways—makes wisdom possible. Fear of the Lord is based on the realization that God exists, that He is the Creator of all things, and that one day we will be accountable to Him for what we have done on the earth.

While many see fear as a negative concept, it is hard to find a better word to convey what we might experience face-to-face with the living God. Certainly God is good, loving, and merciful, and for that reason He can be trusted, but who can truly ponder His almighty power and completely escape some degree of terror? To some extent it is similar to standing at the foot of Niagara Falls or at the edge of the Grand Canyon—what you see before you is awesome and magnificent, but its power and greatness make your stomach lurch at the same time, even though you are perfectly safe.

FEAR OF THE LORD—RESPECTING GOD AND FOLLOWING HIS WAYS—MAKES WISDOM POSSIBLE.

This fear of the Lord is the beginning of wisdom because it is the only thing that can shake a human being out of self-deception and conceit. Some believe in God but without a healthy fear that He is all powerful and an uncompromising righteous judge, so they experience no need to obey Him. To fear God is to make Him Lord of your life and acknowledge that He defines and controls the universe—all knowledge is subject to His truth.

The fear of the Lord also provides a place of perspective from which to judge correctly. Proverbs 8:13 says, "The fear of the Lord is hatred of evil." The person who hates evil will not tolerate it in his life and will do whatever is necessary to avoid it. In everything he does, the wise person judges things from God's perspective, with a regard for the eternal, and therefore he avoids falling into the trap of compromise. With this perspective, things can be judged correctly; without it, all can seem relative, and right and wrong can be easily corrupted by self-deception, conceit, and selfish desire.

> THE BETTER YOU KNOW GOD AND UNDERSTAND HIS WAYS, THE MORE CLEARLY YOU WILL UNDERSTAND THE SITUATIONS AROUND YOU AND KNOW WHAT IS RIGHT NO MATTER THE CIRCUMSTANCES.

Another result of fearing God is having insight, the ability to know where facts fit in with truth. As Solomon wrote, "The fear of the Lord is the beginning of wisdom, and the knowledge of the Holy One is insight" (Proverbs 9:10). With insight you can apply knowledge correctly. The better you know God and understand His ways, the more clearly you will understand the situations around you and know what is right no matter the circumstances.

INSTRUCTION AND DISCIPLINE

Sometimes doing what is right is more a matter of strength of will and purpose than simply knowing what is the right and best thing to do. Without the support of proper habits and abilities that come through training and discipline, knowledge isn't enough.

Let's say that you play golf and you are trying to develop your tee shot. What a good tee shot looks like is pretty easy to visualize; however, you also need the training and muscle memory to execute the shot correctly. First of all, you need to learn the correct swing. Videos, books, or a personal coach can help you develop your stroke. Then you need hours and hours of practice to repeat that stroke precisely over and over, until it is drilled into your muscle memory and you can do it correctly without thinking about it. You also may need more body strength or flexibility that will come only through exercise and stretching.

Solomon understood the necessity of a teachable spirit and being open to instruction and discipline if we want to live with wisdom. He had had the wonderful experience of learning from his father, David. "He who scorns instruction will pay for it," Solomon wrote, "but he who respects a command is rewarded" (Proverbs 13:13 NIV).

Implementing what we learn about wise living can take practice. As in learning a sport, performing as you desire will take discipline until you get it right. If you train and practice when there is no pressure, you'll be ready to be victorious in a pressure-packed game. As Jesus said, "He who is faithful in a very little thing is faithful also in much; and he who is unrighteous in a very little thing is unrighteous also in much" (Luke 16:10 NASB).

THE BETTER YOU KNOW GOD AND UNDERSTAND HIS WAYS, THE MORE CLEARLY YOU WILL UNDERSTAND THE SITUATIONS AROUND YOU AND KNOW WHAT IS RIGHT, NO MATTER THE CIRCUMSTANCES.

Now perhaps you are not big into athletics, but the principle applies in other realms of life as well. If you are sloppy with your finances when things are good, what will happen when you hit a crisis? If you are not faithful in your day-to-day work, what will happen when your job or promotion depends on completing a special project or landing a particular client? If you are lazy in your homework, how will you do on your tests? Some get by on their knowledge for a time, but without diligence and discipline, long-term success eludes them. Paul exhorts in 1 Timothy 4:7 NASB, "...discipline yourself for the purpose of godliness." In life, we sometimes need motivation to do what we know is best. We have to see how we will benefit. For example, it is easy to make a commitment to eat no dessert after the evening meal when we just ate and we're full. But what about the next evening, when someone shows up with our favorite cheesecake? At that point, we need some deeper motivation. Even if we pass the test and don't succumb to the temptation, 1 Timothy 4:8 says that discipline of the body only amounts to a small gain. But when we exercise discipline for the purpose of godliness, we are promised great gain for this life and the next.

When we choose to place the well-being of our spirits above the desires of our flesh for the sake of pleasing God, we will reap great satisfaction and reward. God understands the concept of offering rewards. He promises great rewards throughout Scripture for those who diligently seek Him and His ways.

If we choose to discipline our time so that we are able to commune with God through His Word and prayer, we will position ourselves to receive godly wisdom. Discipline is key for anyone who wants to acquire the knowledge of wisdom that will bring lasting success:

> *Whoever loves discipline loves knowledge,*
> *but he who hates reproof is stupid.*
> PROVERBS 12:1

Putting It All Together

The heart of Solomon's prayer was a request for wisdom. God was pleased to grant Solomon's request, and for years Solomon reigned with reverence for God, receiving His instruction and exercising discipline and discernment. Later in his life, however, Solomon chose to live without God. He wrote about his experimentation in the book of Ecclesiastes, concluding that living without God is futility and meaninglessness, no matter what pleasures are experienced. As Solomon lost his fear of the Lord, his wisdom turned to self-loathing and bitter existentialism.

Prayer and God's Word are our best protection against Solomon's failure in his later years. As we spend time with the Father, He gives us His perspective—we suddenly see clearly what we should do because He has imparted to us that wonderful gift, wisdom.

A Prayer for Godly Wisdom

Father,

In the name of Jesus, I come before you to praise you for the glory of your wisdom.

Lord, I ask you to reveal this wisdom to me as I fellowship with you in prayer, read and meditate on your Word, and study it together with other believers. Open my eyes to the power of your Scriptures and light my path through every decision of my day. May your voice be unmistakable in my heart at all times, and may my every action reflect your love, insight, and righteous judgment.

Help me to realize that disciplining myself for the sake of pleasing you is always worth the price I may have to pay. Help me to see things through eternal eyes, knowing that the rewards I will have when I see you face-to-face far outweigh any sacrifice made on earth. Amen.

SOLOMON'S LIFE SECRET #7: GET WISDOM

Wisdom is foundational, and there is only one place to find it—God himself! As you draw near to God, acknowledging Him as Lord of your life and seeking His direction, He will impart His perspective to you. You will know what is the right and best thing to do at the right time. This is true wisdom, and God wants you to have it.

> *For the LORD gives wisdom;*
> *from his mouth come knowledge and understanding;*
> *he stores up sound wisdom for the upright;*
> *he is a shield to those who walk in integrity,*
> *guarding the paths of justice*
> *and watching over the way of his saints.*
> *Then you will understand righteousness and justice*
> *and equity, every good path;*
> *for wisdom will come into your heart,*
> *and knowledge will be pleasant to your soul;*
> *discretion will watch over you,*
> *understanding will guard you.*
> PROVERBS 2:6-11

WORDS TO LIVE BY

wisdom

1: accumulated philosophic or scientific learning; knowledge
2: ability to discern inner qualities and relationships; insight
3: good sense: judgment

> *[Wisdom] is more precious than jewels,*
> *and nothing you desire can compare with her.*
> *Long life is in her right hand;*
> *in her left hand are riches and honor.* PROVERBS 3:15-16

discern

1: to recognize or identify as separate and distinct; discriminate <discern right from wrong>
2: to come to know or recognize mentally <able to discern his motives>

> *Whoever gives thought to the word will discover good,*
> *and blessed is he who trusts in the* LORD.
> *The wise of heart is called discerning,*
> *and sweetness of speech increases persuasiveness.*
> PROVERBS 16:20-21

VIII·
How to Open Heaven

It pleased the Lord that Solomon had asked this.

1 Kings 3:10

His father's dream of a permanent dwelling place for the Lord in Jerusalem was no longer a dream. As on the day at Gibeon when Solomon watched the smoke rise from the last of his thousand sacrifices at the tabernacle, today he watched the smoke lift from the altar of the Lord in the temple, after sacrifices that were too many to be counted. The temple! Now it had been completed, down to the last detail.

With the elders of Israel, Solomon watched as the priests entered the temple bearing the Ark of the Covenant and all the sacred furnishings from the tabernacle. All stood solemnly as the priests positioned the ark in the Most Holy Place under the wings of the cherubim.

As the priests came out to join the others, a thick, billowing cloud began to fill the temple with the glory of God. The priests could not continue standing to minister because of the glory of God's presence in the temple Solomon had built.

"The Lord has said that He would dwell in the thick cloud," Solomon spoke out to the assembly. "I have surely built You a lofty house, a place for Your dwelling forever" (1 Kings 8:12-13 NASB).

Solomon blessed the assembly standing there and then knelt before the altar with his hands outstretched toward heaven and prayed. At the conclusion of his prayer, he stood and blessed the assembly again in a loud voice:

> *Blessed be the LORD, who has given rest to His people Israel, according to all that He promised; not one word has failed of all His good promise, which He promised through Moses His servant. May the LORD our God be with us, as He was with our fathers; may He not leave us or forsake us, that He may incline our hearts to Himself, to walk in all His ways and to keep His commandments and His statutes and His ordinances, which He commanded our fathers. And may these words of mine, with which I have made supplication before the LORD, be near to the LORD our God day and night, that He may maintain the cause of His servant and the cause of His people Israel, as each day requires, so that all the peoples*

> *of the earth may know that the LORD is God; there is no one*
> *else. Let your heart therefore be wholly devoted to the LORD*
> *our God, to walk in His statutes and to keep His command-*
> *ments, as at this day.*
> 1 KINGS 8:56-61 NASB

The dedication of the temple continued with more sacrifices and two weeks of feasting. Then the people blessed the king and joyfully returned to their homes, mindful of all the good things the Lord had done for Israel.

The day of dedicating the temple to the Lord was Solomon's greatest achievement, and it had all started at Gibeon in a prayer that showed a heart pleasing to God. Because Solomon asked in humility for wisdom that he might serve as a just ruler for the people of Israel, God was willing to open up all the good things of heaven to him as well: peace, prosperity, long life, and honor. If we are willing to submit to and seek God, then the same things are open to us.

SOLOMON AT HIS BEST

During the first decade or so of his rule, Solomon's allegiance was clearly to heaven, his father's legacy, and living out all God had given him the wisdom to do. When God was first, all good things followed.

God confirmed his pleasure with Solomon after he finished the new house for himself and his family—He came again to Solomon as He had at Gibeon. Solomon had accomplished all that his father, David, hoped he would, but what would be Solomon's own legacy? What was he going to do to follow his own purpose and destiny? Was it time for Solomon to sit back and enjoy life now, or was it time to renew his purpose and seek greater things with God?

When God came this time, He did not simply endorse what Solomon had accomplished to that point. He also warned him of danger ahead, the danger of growing complacent:

> *If you turn aside from following me, you or your children, and do not keep my commandments and my statutes that I have set before you, but go and serve other gods and worship them, then I will cut off Israel from the land that I have given them, and the house that I have consecrated for my name I will cast out of my sight, and Israel will become a proverb and a byword among all peoples. And this house will become a heap of ruins. Everyone passing by it will be astonished and will hiss, and they will say, "Why has the LORD done thus to this land and to this*

> house?" Then they will say, "Because they abandoned the
> LORD their God who brought their fathers out of the land
> of Egypt and laid hold on other gods and worshiped them
> and served them. Therefore the LORD has brought all this
> disaster on them."
>
> 1 KINGS 9:6-9

Unfortunately, Solomon did not heed God's warning. The end of Solomon's life was marked by falling away and not by continued devotion and integrity before God. In the remaining decades of his rule after he had fulfilled the dreams of his father, Solomon carved out a legacy that would be remembered not only for its heights and successes but also for its depths of despair and ultimate failure.

SOLOMON'S FOLLY

Solomon failed to stay the course and fulfill all God had for him. While we have some of his best wisdom recorded in the book of Proverbs, we also have his deep despair recorded in the book of Ecclesiastes, which speaks of a life that began in glory and ended in emptiness, futility, disillusionment, and vanity because Solomon's heart had fallen away from God.

Despite being the wisest man who ever lived, Solomon

did not escape the trappings of sin. He did not fulfill the stipulations of God's promise to his father by walking before the Lord in faithfulness and integrity with all his heart and all his soul to the end of his days. Though the kingdom was spared during his lifetime—again for the sake of his father, David—Solomon's son Rehoboam, who took the throne after Solomon's death, did not inherit his father's early wisdom or humility. Perhaps Solomon lost his desire to raise his children as David had raised him. Rehoboam so enraged the people of Israel with his lack of mercy and compassion that the nation was ripped in two in a bloodless coup. Every other tribe of Israel rebelled against Judah and broke away to form the northern kingdom of Israel.

GREAT ACCOMPLISHMENTS ARE SELDOM DEFEATED BY GREAT RESISTANCE, BUT OVERCOME DAY IN AND DAY OUT BY SELFISH, SMALL DISTRACTIONS.

Why did Solomon, who really had it all, fail after so great a beginning?

Great accomplishments are seldom defeated by great resistance, but are overcome day in and day out by selfish, small distractions. After over twenty years of blessed and righteous rule, the Scriptures tell us, Solomon began to compromise his heart for the sake of comfort and pleasure:

> *Now King Solomon loved many foreign women, along with the daughter of Pharaoh: Moabite, Ammonite, Edomite,*

> Sidonian, and Hittite women, from the nations concerning
> which the LORD had said to the people of Israel, "You shall
> not enter into marriage with them, neither shall they with
> you, for surely they will turn away your heart after their
> gods." Solomon clung to these in love. He had 700 wives,
> princesses, and 300 concubines. And his wives turned away
> his heart. For when Solomon was old his wives turned away
> his heart after other gods, and his heart was not wholly true
> to the LORD his God, as was the heart of David his father.
> 1 KINGS 11:1-4

And his own writings in the book of Ecclesiastes tell us:

> I said in my heart, "Come now, I will test you with pleasure;
> enjoy yourself." . . . I searched with my heart how to cheer my
> body with wine—my heart still guiding me with wisdom—
> and how to lay hold on folly, till I might see what was good
> for the children of man to do under heaven during the few
> days of their life. I made great works. I built houses and
> planted vineyards for myself. I made myself gardens and
> parks, and planted in them all kinds of fruit trees. I made
> myself pools from which to water the forest of growing trees. I
> bought male and female slaves, and had slaves who were born
> in my house. I had also great possessions of herds and flocks,
> more than any who had been before me in Jerusalem. I also
> gathered for myself silver and gold and the treasure of kings

and provinces. I got singers, both men and women, and many concubines, the delight of the children of man.

So I became great and surpassed all who were before me in Jerusalem. Also my wisdom remained with me. And whatever my eyes desired I did not keep from them. I kept my heart from no pleasure, for my heart found pleasure in all my toil, and this was my reward for all my toil. Then I considered all that my hands had done and the toil I had expended in doing it, and behold, all was vanity and a striving after wind, and there was nothing to be gained under the sun.
ECCLESIASTES 2:1, 3-11

Solomon's downfall was that he turned his pursuit from the things of God to the things of this world. His purpose turned from the prosperity and well-being of others to the unhindered pursuit of his own pleasures and desires. Distracted by his foreign wives and concubines, he sought to please them rather than God. He built shrines near Jerusalem where his wives could burn incense and offer sacrifices to their pagan gods, and he worshiped their gods himself. By doing so, Solomon opened the door in Israel to the worship of false gods, and that soon caused the people to turn their backs on all that had made them great.

Greatness in life is better defined by the value of what we

are pursuing than by what we accomplish. When Solomon pursued God with all his heart, Israel was blessed by God. When he pursued his own comfort and satisfaction and turned away from God, he destroyed the nation's foundation.

GREATNESS IN LIFE IS BETTER DEFINED BY THE VALUE OF WHAT WE ARE PURSUING THAN BY WHAT WE ACCOMPLISH.

Could Solomon's ultimate failure become our own?

All that lasts is not made of brick and mortar or commendations and bonuses but what our lives inspire in the hearts of others. Do you impassion others to wholeheartedly pursue the destiny and purpose God has for them? Or do you provide an excuse for others to spend their days in compromise and comfort-seeking that will ultimately waste the time, talents, and treasures God has given them to steward?

SOLOMON'S FINAL LESSON

Solomon's heart turned from God, and his final words are not of a life fulfilled and heavenly rewards obtained but of bitterness and emptiness. Distracted from pursuing God by the pleasures of this world, Solomon fell into despair and led the nation into disrepair, leading ultimately to the exile of God's people in foreign lands.

Solomon did not fail in hearing God's voice but in obeying what he heard. That is his final lesson for us. When God went to Solomon at Gibeon and offered him whatever he might ask for, Solomon made the best choice and asked for wisdom instead of riches, long life, or the death of his enemies. However, he had already made two other choices early in his reign that were unwise and that ultimately opened the door to his falling away from God later in his life.

The first unwise choice had to do with the worship practices of Israel. When Solomon wanted to seek God and offer his one thousand sacrifices, he went to the tabernacle, the tent of meeting that God told Moses to construct when the Israelites were wandering in the desert. When Solomon began his reign, the tabernacle was located at Gibeon, "the great high place" (1 Kings 3:4). A high place was a place of worship to pagan gods; the Israelites had never completely eradicated the worship of false gods from their land and periodically fell into the worship of false gods themselves. God had clearly commanded that He alone should be worshiped; yet Scripture tells us that Solomon allowed the high places to remain when he became king. (See 1 Kings 3:3-4.)

Solomon's second unwise choice early in his reign was his marriage to Pharaoh's daughter, which sealed an alliance Solomon had made with Egypt (1 Kings 3:1). As we have already seen, God had clearly warned the Israelites not to intermarry with the people of the nations from which these women came, because He knew that doing so would eventually lead the hearts of His people away from Him.

God allowed these acts of Solomon's to stand. Despite Solomon's disobedience, God still went to him at Gibeon, offering to give him whatever he might ask for. These early unwise choices Solomon had made might have been undone if Solomon had been willing to examine his heart and motives completely. Instead, despite Solomon's clear love for God and strong desire to do His will, it seems that he kept a secret place in his heart walled off from God. The choices Solomon made that sprung from that walled-off, unexamined place early in his life grew slowly and quietly throughout his reign. Finally, he had hundreds of foreign wives and concubines and had begun to worship their false gods himself.

It is interesting that when God gave His laws to the Israelites before they entered the Promised Land, He told them:

> When you come to the land that the LORD your God is giving you, and you possess it and dwell in it and then say, "I will set

> *a king over me, like all the nations that are around me," you may indeed set a king over you whom the* LORD *your God will choose. . . . Only he must not acquire many horses for himself or cause the people to return to Egypt in order to acquire many horses, since the* LORD *has said to you, "You shall never return that way again." And he shall not acquire many wives for himself, lest his heart turn away, nor shall he acquire for himself excessive silver and gold.*
>
> DEUTERONOMY 17:14-17

Although Solomon did not look to Egypt for help to defend his country, as some of the kings who followed him did do, he did ally himself with Egypt, and he did buy horses from Egypt. (See 1 Kings 10:28.) He also chose to ignore God's command, in the passage above, not to have many wives.

Solomon's final lesson for us, then, is the impact of our choices. No matter how inconsequential we may think our choices might be, when it comes to obeying God, there really are no small choices; every choice we make to obey or disobey has a big impact on our lives and the lives of others. Jesus spoke about this when He said to His disciples, "Unless you are faithful in small matters, you won't be faithful in large ones. If you cheat even a little, you won't be honest with greater responsibilities" (Luke 16:10 NLT).

Sometimes we can deceive ourselves by thinking that as long as we do most of what God says, it is okay to let a few things slide every now and then. We tend to categorize wrongdoings by our estimation of worth. Unfortunately, what we think are small offenses may end up making a huge difference in our lives. God sees the big picture, and He knows us better than we know ourselves. When He instructs us to do something or to specifically avoid doing something, He has a good reason. We must obey Him even when it seems trivial to us. And we must obey Him even when we see other Christians doing just the opposite.

WHEN IT COMES TO OBEYING GOD, THERE REALLY ARE NO SMALL CHOICES; EVERY CHOICE WE MAKE TO OBEY OR DISOBEY HAS A BIG IMPACT ON OUR LIVES AND THE LIVES OF OTHERS.

Obedience is the key in small matters as well as large ones. In Solomon's life, we see the end result of allowing our obedience to become selective. Let's take seriously his mistakes so that we don't end our own lives with similar regret.

However, as disheartening as Solomon's last days were, it would be foolish to discard the lessons of Solomon's early life. The marks of his prayer at Gibeon—gratitude and humility, his heart for God, his embrace of his life's purpose, and the pursuit of wisdom—are to be clung to, not dismissed. Solomon's wisdom is preserved for us in the Bible because it was not his wisdom that failed. Instead, even though he knew better, Solomon allowed himself to turn from righteousness and integrity to selfish pursuits and pleasure seeking, and in so doing, he traded in his greater destiny.

How to Stay True

What about us? Many receive the gift of salvation but few allow God full sway in their lives. Obedience must be pursued continually toward God's ultimate purpose for saving us in the first place. Look at how Paul put this to the Philippians:

> Therefore, my dear friends, as you have always obeyed—not only in my presence, but now much more in my absence—continue to work out your salvation with fear and trembling, for it is God who works in you to will and to act according to his good purpose. . . .
>
> Not that I have already obtained all this, or have already been made perfect, but I press on to take hold of that for which Christ Jesus took hold of me. Brothers, I do not consider myself yet to have taken hold of it. But one thing I do: Forgetting what is behind and straining toward what is

> *ahead, I press on toward the goal to win the prize for which*
> *God has called me heavenward in Christ Jesus.*
> Philippians 2:12-13; 3:12-14 NIV

Paul makes it clear that remaining faithful to God is a life-long pursuit, requiring action on our part. God has promised that He will do His part to bring us into His kingdom and He will keep His promise (2 Timothy 4:18). What then are some of the ways we can do our part to ensure we will be found faithful to Him at the end of our lives on earth?

The first action we need to take is to know God's Word. Don't make the mistake of limiting your Bible reading to a passage here and there as part of studying a lesson or reading a devotional book. While there is nothing bad about either of these kinds of reading, neither one is enough to help you stay true to God for the rest of your life. God wants you to know Him, and He desires to reveal himself to you through His Word each and every day. Contrary to any misconceptions you may have, you can understand the Bible. Three chapters a day will take you through the entire Bible in a year, and there are many different reading plans and chronological arrangements to help you. Although some events in your reading may puzzle you when you encounter them for the first time, as you continue to read and get to know the character of God, you will discover that you understand more and more of what you read. Moses told the Israelites, "Real life comes by feeding on every word of the LORD" (Deuteronomy 8:3 NLT). As you set aside a time each day to commune with God by reading His Word, God will reveal himself and His plan to you. He will impart the particular strength and grace that will be needed for that day.

THE FIRST ACTION WE NEED TO TAKE IS TO KNOW GOD'S WORD.

Although reading and studying God's Word is crucial to survival for the Christian, if you stop there, you've missed part of the equation. What is the other part? To do God's Word! We must not only read God's Word, but we must also seek to actively apply it.

> Do not merely listen to the word, and so deceive yourselves. Do what it says. Anyone who listens to the word but does not do what it says is like a man who looks at his face in a mirror and, after looking at himself, goes away and immediately forgets what he looks like. But the man who looks intently into the perfect law that gives freedom, and continues to do this, not forgetting what he has heard, but doing it—he will be blessed in what he does.
>
> JAMES 1:22-25 NIV

From the passage above, we can see that God expects us to obey what He says. This is one of the reasons that Solomon's life ended in failure. He did not obey the Lord wholeheartedly, as was mentioned previously. God's Word is our guide and we should take it literally.

A second action we can take to help us stay true is to choose to live our lives connected to other believers, rather than trying to live a Christian life in isolation. Solomon's last days might have turned out differently if his closest relationships were with others who cared greatly about the choices he made. Have you ever thought about why there are so many "one anothers" in the New Testament? We need other Christians who know us well to rejoice with us when life is good, to pray for us when we sin, and to help us carry our heavy burdens. "Bear one another's burdens, and so fulfill the law of Christ" (Galatians 6:2).

Peter wrote that when believers use the gifts we have been given to serve others, we are "administering God's grace in its various forms" (1 Peter 4:10 NIV). In other words, one of the most important ways God blesses and helps us is through other believers. All Christians are a part of Christ's body (Romans 12:5), and we need one another.

Getting a clear picture of the reality of the world we live

in is a third action we should take if we want to stay true.

As John Eldredge wrote in *Waking the Dead*, "Things are not what they seem. This is a world at war." We have an enemy whose chief aim is to destroy us. God has given us armor and weapons to use to stand against Satan, but we are not inclined to use those if we aren't convinced that the battle is real.

A SECOND ACTION WE CAN TAKE TO HELP US STAY TRUE IS TO CHOOSE TO LIVE OUR LIVES CONNECTED TO OTHER BELIEVERS.

God tells us to wear and use His armor so that we can "stand firm" (Ephesians 6:14 NIV). Paul wrote, "Our struggle is not against flesh and blood, but against the rulers, against the authorities, against the powers of this dark world and against the spiritual forces of evil in the heavenly realms" (Ephesians 6:12 NIV). We need to understand that although God has already won the war, the battles will continue until Christ returns. If we want to stay true to God throughout our lives, we need to live each day believing that and acting like we believe it.

THE LIFE GOD REWARDS

God is a rewarder of those who seek His wisdom, for by it the world was created, the universe set into motion, and all spiritual laws put into place. On the surface, wisdom may seem nothing but common sense, but by humbling ourselves to look more deeply and study more ardently, wisdom will begin to give up its secrets. It is like honey to our souls.

> *My son, eat honey, for it is good,*
> *and the drippings of the honeycomb are sweet to your taste.*
> *Know that wisdom is such to your soul;*
> *if you find it, there will be a future,*
> *and your hope will not be cut off.*
> PROVERBS 24:13-14

It is through God's wisdom that we lay out the blueprints for our futures in our every action. By it we plan and prepare; we keep our priorities straight. Wisdom is like the true north of a compass: Without it all our bearings have no meaning. With wisdom, however, although we may not know what is on the other side of the mountain, we can know what direction in which to proceed.

Wisdom opens heaven over us for our open hearts to receive. It informs our faith and gives confidence and action to our beliefs. It is by wisdom that we come to the knowledge of the truth and bring others to it as well.

It is wisdom that establishes your house and fills

it with the goodness of God.

> By wisdom a house is built,
> and by understanding it is established;
> by knowledge the rooms are filled
> with all precious and pleasant riches.
> A wise man is full of strength,
> and a man of knowledge enhances his might,
> for by wise guidance you can wage your war,
> and in abundance of counselors there is victory.
> PROVERBS 24:3-6

If we are to learn anything from the prayer of Solomon, it is that all blessings in life are a by-product of acting according to God's wisdom, seeking Him first above all else. Fulfillment comes through following God's purpose for us. If we will follow His leading with a servant's heart, He will do through us greater things than we have ever hoped or imagined. This is living the life that God rewards, seeking Him and the establishment of His kingdom before anything else.

One of the great mysteries of God is that today is always the best day to begin any journey searching for Him. This is the day to begin your pursuit of all God has for you. Apply what you have learned here through Solomon's prayer, guard your heart with the good attitudes he portrayed, and adopt the confidence of a child who knows his Father's desire for him. You will find fulfillment by following the pattern of Solomon's prayer and walking according to God's Spirit all the days of your life.

Godspeed in your journey toward discovering His best for your life.

A Prayer of Commitment

Father,

I come to you in Jesus' name with the openness and obedience of a little child. You have called me to be your ambassador on this planet, and you have entrusted me with your light and truth to deliver others from the foolishness and pride of this age.

Please give me your wisdom to walk in all my days. Help me to stay true to you and your ways my whole life long. Give me an understanding mind to touch others and bring them to a saving knowledge of you and your Son, Jesus.

Amen.

Solomon's Life Secret #8: Stay true

Solomon was the wisest man who ever lived upon the earth—he was blessed with honor, a long life, and riches. But his life ended in bitterness and disillusionment. Why? Because he lost his first love. He began his rule with a heart that chased after God; his allegiance was to God and no one else. But after God rewarded him, he began to seek the rewards and not God. He followed after riches and pleasure and forsook God. The latter part of his life revealed a life not lived by wisdom. His heart had turned from the true source of wisdom—God.

As you leave this study of Solomon's prayer, set your heart to seek God's face and presence as Solomon once did, not just His hand that brings you blessings. Let His purpose possess you and direct you. Let His Word be a lamp to your feet, and follow His Spirit. Allow His abundant life to flow into you and from you so that you can be the blessing He intended you to be.

> The LORD bless you, and keep you;
> The LORD make His face shine on you,
> And be gracious to you;
> The LORD lift up His countenance on you,
> And give you peace.
>
> Numbers 6:24-26 NASB

Words to Live By

allegiance

1: the fidelity owed by a subject or citizen to a sovereign or government
2: devotion or loyalty to a person, group, or cause

> Turn to me and be saved, all the ends of the earth!
> For I am God, and there is no other.
> By myself I have sworn; from my mouth has gone out in righteousness a word that shall not return:
> "To me every knee shall bow, every tongue shall swear allegiance." ISAIAH 45:22-23

reward

1: something that is given in return for good or evil done or received or that is offered or given for some service or attainment

> Without faith it is impossible to please him, for whoever would draw near to God must believe that he exists and that he rewards those who seek him. HEBREWS 11:6

The Wise Sayings of Solomon About Trusting the Lord

Trust in the LORD with all your heart
and lean not on your own understanding;
in all your ways acknowledge him,
and he will make your paths straight.
  PROVERBS 3:5-6 NIV

Do not be afraid of sudden fear
Nor of the onslaught of the wicked when it comes;
For the LORD will be your confidence
And will keep your foot from being caught.
PROVERBS 3:25-26 NASB

Trust in your money and down you go!
But the godly flourish like leaves in spring.
  PROVERBS 11:28 NLT

Whoever gives heed to instruction prospers,
and blessed is he who trusts in the LORD.
PROVERBS 16:20 NIV

Don't try to get even. Trust the LORD,
and he will help you.
PROVERBS 20:22 CEV

The Lord Is My Confidence

Trust is such a simple word, yet it can be so difficult to implement.

We live in such a dysfunctional society these days that it almost seems foolish to trust anyone.

But God says over and over again that He wants us to trust Him. So how do we do that? A good starting place is to study God's character. The Bible says He is loyal, trustworthy, loving, kind, generous, and wise. The Bible also says there is no evil within Him at all. Reflect on that idea for a moment. You may even want to memorize a Scripture or two on the attributes that are most meaningful to you.

The next time that you are in a struggle and are tempted to believe that God is just like every person you know who has let you down, remember and meditate on what you studied. Speak the Scripture you memorized out loud to yourself and make a decision that this once you will trust in Him.

See if He doesn't come through for you. He will prove himself trustworthy if you just give Him a chance. Why not start today?

The Wise Sayings of Solomon About Being a Peacemaker

Smart people know how to hold their tongue;
their grandeur is to forgive and forget.
PROVERBS 19:11 THE MESSAGE

Keeping away from strife is an honor for a man,
But any fool will quarrel.
PROVERBS 20:3 NASB

Starting a quarrel is like breaching a dam;
so drop the matter before a dispute breaks out.
PROVERBS 17:14 NIV

A hothead starts fights;
a cool-tempered person tries to stop them.
PROVERBS 15:18 NLT

Drive out the mocker, and out goes strife;
quarrels and insults are ended.
PROVERBS 22:10 NIV

Plugging the Leak!

How to avoid strife—that is a lesson we can all glean from! The Bible gives much insight on the subject. In one instance it compares strife to water and says not to let it get out of hand. Isn't that an accurate picture? Once strife gets started, it is hard to stop. Another Scripture says that avoiding strife brings honor. That is because God is pleased when we choose not to argue when everything within us screams that we are justified in doing so.

It appears then, that in avoiding strife, we need to be careful of two things. We should not start it. And if someone else starts it, we should be quick to stop it.

In the first case, the Bible warns that harsh words can stir up anger. Harsh words cause us to get on the defensive, and then we're ready to strike back. Strife can become an endless cycle of people trading insult for insult.

In the second case, it means that we must swallow our pride and make the decision that it doesn't matter who is to blame; we are going to take the high road. God is honored when, for His sake, we choose to be peacemakers.

The Wise Sayings of Solomon on Diligence & Hard Work

He who works his land will have abundant food,
but he who chases fantasies lacks judgment.
Proverbs 12:11 niv

He who has a slack hand becomes poor,
But the hand of the diligent makes rich.
He who gathers in summer is a wise son;
He who sleeps in harvest is a son who causes shame.
Proverbs 10:4-5 nkjv

In all labor there is profit,
But mere talk leads only to poverty.
Proverbs 14:23 nasb

Do you see a man skilled in his work?
He will serve before kings;
he will not serve before obscure men.
Proverbs 22:29 niv

The plans of the diligent lead to profit
as surely as haste leads to poverty.
Proverbs 21:5 niv

BIG "D" PAYS BIG TIME!

Diligence is defined by the *Random House Unabridged Dictionary* as "a constant and earnest effort to accomplish what is undertaken; persistent exertion of body or mind."

Solomon, the wisest person who ever lived, aside from Jesus, spoke a lot about diligence in the book of Proverbs. It is a character trait that pleases God and one that brings great reward.

How would you rate yourself on the diligence scale? Do you seek to do your best no matter how menial the task? Or do you do just enough to get by? Do you feel some tasks are beneath you?

Any job done with all your strength will boost your self-esteem. You can have the inner satisfaction of knowing that you did your best. It also can bring other rewards. Your employer may notice and promote you. But whether he or she notices or not, there is Someone else who always takes note. Your hard work never goes unnoticed or unrewarded by God. He promises that if you are faithful in small things, big things will come later.

So, don't quit; don't give up. Rather, put your whole heart into whatever and wherever God has you at this time. The extra effort will be worth it!

The Wise Sayings of Solomon About Self-Control

Slowness to anger makes for deep understanding;
a quick-tempered person stockpiles stupidity.
Proverbs 14:29 the message

Better a patient man than a warrior,
a man who controls his temper than one who takes a city.
Proverbs 16:32 niv

A man of great anger will bear the penalty,
For if you rescue him, you will only have to do it again.
Proverbs 19:19 nasb

He who loves pleasure will become poor;
whoever loves wine and oil will never be rich.
Proverbs 21:17 niv

A fool gives full vent to his anger,
but a wise man keeps himself under control.
Proverbs 29:11 niv

Just Say No

Self-control is definitely not one of our favorite topics. It is so painful to say no to ourselves, isn't it?

By allowing God to cultivate this character trait within us, we reap great rewards. For example, when we say no to the second helping of mashed potatoes, tomorrow we will be glad when our pants still fit. And when we decide to forego that thirty-minute sitcom, the next morning we will be rejoicing when we feel rested for the day.

On the other hand, when we fail to set limitations on ourselves, we reap the negative effects. How many of us have lost our tempers, only minutes later to regret the pain and shame it brought us and others. And who hasn't winced in pain when that overdraft notice from the bank came in the mail. We've all been there!

Instead of seeing self-control as a deprivation, we just need to change our thinking. We need to realize all the benefits it affords us. God wants us to have happy, fulfilled lives, and He knows that reigning ourselves in sometimes is the only way to achieve that. Say no to yourself today!

The Wise Sayings of Solomon on the Fear of the Lord

The fear of the LORD is the beginning of wisdom,
And the knowledge of the Holy One is understanding.
Proverbs. 9:10 nasb

Fear of the LORD gives life, security,
 and protection from harm.
Proverbs 19:23 nlt

Fear of the LORD lengthens one's life,
but the years of the wicked are cut short.
Proverbs 10:27 nlt

Do not be wise in your own eyes;
fear the LORD and shun evil.
Proverbs 3:7 niv

A simple life in the Fear-of-God
is better than a rich life with a ton of headaches.
Proverbs 15:16 the message

LIFE-GIVING FEAR

The Bible says that the fear of the Lord is the beginning of wisdom. So the fear of the Lord is foundational. But what is it exactly?

The fear of the Lord involves standing in awe of God. It is the realization that He is the one and only God and that we owe Him our undivided allegiance. It is the understanding that our lives do not belong to us—we do not stand alone as a separate entity accountable only to ourselves. In fact, we owe our very breath to God, for Scripture tells us that in Him we actually live and move and have our being. (See Acts 17:28.)

So how does this translate into everyday living? For the Christian, it means that we should acknowledge God in everything, great or small. It means we should submit to His will for our lives because He is our Creator and has the right to direct us. And because He is also our Father who loves us dearly, we have an even greater motivation to obey Him.

The fear of the Lord leads us to the true source of wisdom, peace, and happiness—God himself.

The Wise Sayings of Solomon on the Power of Words

A gentle answer turns away wrath,
but a harsh word stirs up anger.
Proverbs 15:1 niv

There is one who speaks rashly like the thrusts of a sword,
But the tongue of the wise brings healing.
Proverbs 12:18 nasb

The more talk, the less truth;
the wise measure their words.
Proverbs 10:19 the message

A wise man's heart guides his mouth,
and his lips promote instruction.
Pleasant words are a honeycomb,
sweet to the soul and healing to the bones.
Proverbs 16:23-24 niv

He who restrains his words has knowledge,
And he who has a cool spirit is a man of understanding.
Even a fool, when he keeps silent, is considered wise;
When he closes his lips, he is considered prudent.
Proverbs 17:27-28 nasb

THE POWER TO BLESS

We've all been the recipients of words that brought pain. On the other hand, we may still have the memory of a supportive word someone gave us when we were struggling. One lifted our spirits while the other put a heavier weight on our already loaded backs.

Because of the tremendous power in words, God devotes many Scriptures to this subject. Not only can our words wield great influence on another, but one day we will also have to give an account to God for all the words we have ever spoken. That's a scary thought, isn't it?

No wonder Solomon told us that the wise person disciplines his tongue, while the fool just says anything that comes to mind. We can either bring words of comfort, encouragement, and grace to others. Or we can bring despair, discouragement, and judgment. The choice is ours.

So let's dedicate our tongues to God. Let's ask Him to help us, by the power of the Holy Spirit, to speak good things into the hearts and lives of the people we come in contact with every day. Let's bless, not curse!

The Wise Sayings of Solomon on Walking in Integrity

The man of integrity walks securely,
but he who takes crooked paths will be found out.
Proverbs 10:9 niv

The integrity of the upright will guide them,
But the crookedness of the treacherous will destroy them.
Proverbs 11:3 nasb

Righteousness guards the man of integrity,
but wickedness overthrows the sinner.
Proverbs 13:6 niv

Better is the poor who walks in his integrity
Than he who is crooked though he be rich.
Proverbs 28:6 nasb

The righteous man walks in his integrity;
His children are blessed after him.
Proverbs 20:7 nkjv

THE INTERNAL COMPASS

Integrity is a word that is often misunderstood. Many of us think it merely means whether or not we steal from others. But real integrity means so much more.

It can also mean whether or not we are honest about who we are at the root level. Sometimes we say one thing when we really mean another. An example of this behavior is laughing at an off-color joke, even though we don't think it is funny, in order to fit in with the crowd. We have just been dishonest with others and ourselves. We sacrificed our true selves on the "altar of acceptance."

Another form of this kind of dishonesty is when we try to emulate the gifts and talents of another. We fail to pull it off because we don't have the goods. The truth is that God has made us unique and we have our own set of gifts and abilities.

Integrity is shown when what's on the inside of us matches what is on the outside. Walking in integrity isn't always easy, but it is satisfying, because the "real person" within us is being affirmed. Why not take a chance today and be the wonderful person God created you to be?